T0078069

MOVE MOUNTAIN: Book Three
Leadership Matters
Politics and Evangelicals
A walk down memory lane
January 21 to June 21, 2017

Dr. Millicent Thomas

Leadership Matters

A Walk Down Memory Lane

Dr. Millicent Thomas

BALBOA.PRESS
A DIVISION OF HAY HOUSE

Balboa Press books may be ordered through booksellers or by contacting:

Balboa Press
A Division of Hay House
1663 Liberty Drive
Bloomington, IN 47403
www.balboapress.com
844-682-1282

Because of the dynamic nature of the Internet, any web addresses or links contained in
this book may have changed since publication and may no longer be valid. The views
expressed in this work are solely those of the author and do not necessarily reflect the
views of the publisher, and the publisher hereby disclaims any responsibility for them.

The author of this book does not dispense medical advice or prescribe the use
of any technique as a form of treatment for physical, emotional, or medical
problems without the advice of a physician, either directly or indirectly. The
intent of the author is only to offer information of a general nature to help you
in your quest for emotional and spiritual well-being. In the event you use any
of the information in this book for yourself, which is your constitutional right,
the author and the publisher assume no responsibility for your actions.

Any people depicted in stock imagery provided by Getty Images are
models, and such images are being used for illustrative purposes only.
Certain stock imagery © Getty Images.

Print information available on the last page.

ISBN: 978-1-9822-5814-6 (sc)
ISBN: 978-1-9822-5813-9 (hc)
ISBN: 978-1-9822-5815-3 (e)

Library of Congress Control Number: 2020922060

Balboa Press rev. date: 12/30/2020

It is my hope that if the current president, Donald J. Trump, or any member of this family pursue political life, that the reader will reflect on the writings in this book as a reminder that Leadership Matters!
Dr. Millicent Thomas

Move Mountain: Leadership Matters
Dedicated to my daughter, Nicole, who has a genuine
heart of kindness and my youngest sister Florence,
(Toni), a true seeker of God's knowledge.

Thank you to my Pastor, Rev. Dr. Ralph, D. West of The Church without Walls, 5725 Queenston Blvd. Houston, Texas 77084, for providing the foundation of *Leadership Matters* and to Dr. Paul Harder for his invaluable contribution to the content of my project: Move Mountain Book Series

CONTENTS

PREFACE

I started writing Leadership Matters the first Sunday, after the 2016 election. I could not believe that we, Americans, had experienced eight years of real or imagined harmony. We still have systemic problems. And given the history of race, class, age, and gender in this country, it seemed that race relations were finally standing in the light. At least a glimmer of light, and for some, we were. We still had police murders, and the NRA had dug in their heels. It just felt better and, when the meanness of US citizens wanted to take center stage, President Barack Obama stood flat-footed and spoke against what was wrong. Leadership is what made the difference. Leadership sets the tone in any organization.

Leadership in The Oxford Dictionary is "The action of leading a group of people or an organization." Academicians, like Dr. Janine Utell of Widener University-Pennsylvania states, "for higher education, leadership should further the purpose of higher education, teach, facilitate learning, promote a vision, develop and innovate new ideas." She suggests that there are qualities that are appropriate for all leaders like, effectively navigate their terrain and speak the appropriate language to the people you serve." Also, according to Utell, "Leadership is not just about getting things done. It is about the people you are leading being convinced you are the right person for the job. And, for academics that means having a sense that the visionary at the front of the room is one of them."

The Business Dictionary states, "Leadership involves: establishing a clear vision, sharing that vision with others so that they will follow willingly, providing the information, knowledge, and methods to realize that vision, and coordinating and balancing the conflicting interests of all members and stakeholders."

A leader steps up in times of crisis and can think and act creatively in difficult situations. Unlike management, leadership cannot be taught. It may be learned and enhanced through coaching or mentoring. Someone with leadership skills in the business arena today is Bill Gates. Despite early failures, with passion and innovation, he has driven Microsoft and the software industry to success. Warren Buffet gave penny stocks a whole new meaning. We can also look to Rev. Al Sharpton and Rev. Barber, who are considered affective oracles who consistently speak against injustices.

But how do you define leadership from a Biblical sense? Jesus said in John 21, verse 17, "Feed my sheep." What does that mean? Some commentators would suggest that it means to care for the weak. I looked to Isaiah (10:1-3), as a further explanation that warms us not to reject the poor and needy, widows and, fatherless. This would have a significant meaning for those in leadership positions.

Throughout Biblical history, we can read about leaders. Solomon did not ask for riches or the disposal of his enemies. He asked for wisdom, understanding, and a discerning heart. We can scroll back in time and see the wisdom of Abraham. Rather than encounter conflict between subordinates, he and his nephew Lott separated from each other.

Brian Williams, the MSNBC 11th Hour News program commentator, asked a very discerning question, "Who can speak truth to power?" The seminal question became an anchor for questioning leadership. Again, God's word through the Bible gives us examples. Sarah was Abraham's wife. Even though she made a mistake, she knew that if siblings were not separated trouble would ensue in years not yet come. Moses had his brother, Aaron, his spokesman, and his father-in-law, Jethro, who recommended that he establish a structure to organize the Israelite people. That structure is often used today in many churches. King David, who is reported to be the apple of God's eye, had the prophet,

Nathan. God used Jerimiah to be His voice to King Josiah, even though the king did not listen.

If we fast forward to worthy leaders in the 20th Century, one of the most famous, was President John F. Kennedy who had his brother, Attorney General Robert Kennedy. The Godly voice of reason for humanity can be seen in the words of Martin Luther King Jr. for both Kennedys and President Lyndon B. Johnson. Even President Ronald Regan had Nancy, his wife and, Ned Regan, the second of three Chief of Staff during his administration who spoke truth to power.

What is also essential for leadership is for a leader to be surrounded by competent people. I would argue that subordinates would be prepared with intelligence, and experts in their disciplines; honest and have the fortitude to speak the truth. They would also have wisdom and discernment.

In reflecting on past president Barak H. Obama, Number 44, and the current president, Donald Trump- Number 45, I can see America moving from being welcomed prisoners of hope into one of the prisoners of despair and wrapped in carnage. This was bluntly stated and witnessed by the entire world on Friday and Saturday, August 11, and 12, 2017 as racist events unfolded and were exacerbated by the Trump press conference held on Tuesday, August 15, 2017.

The hope that was once projected by the Obama administration resulted in tangible outcomes for millions in affordable health care; financial assistance for homeownership through the Home Affordable Refinance Program (HARP); keeping the doors of General Motors open, and the list of intangible hope to tangible hope was almost diminished by a president who was waiting to put pen to paper to sign a document intended to hurt and disable millions of Americans.

As a child, I often heard a popular notion; "If you dig one ditch, you'd better dig two. The same ditch you dig just may be for you." America is on the world stage. All countries are watching, and I am sure they are asking, Is this real? Is this America? Christians may be asking, is this God's plan? This is a rhetorical question as there is no answer for no one can determine God's plan. If the administration chooses to execute behavior that challenges leaders of other countries, or disparages opponents, it is much like digging a ditch. What you and I can do is recognize and understand that as the hymn of yesteryears says, "We will understand it better by and by." In this learning process, we begin to understand that leadership truly matters.

The first stanza of a song written by C. A. Tindley (date unknown) states:

> "We are often tossed and driven on the reckless sea of time,
> Somber skies and howling tempest oft succeed the bright sunshine,
> In that land of a perfect day, when the mists have rolled away,
> We will understand it better by and by."

CHAPTER ONE

Introduction

The recognition of leadership history, presidential leadership, and Biblical references is a significant aspect in this first chapter. This chapter lays the foundation for reassurance that there is nothing new under the sun. Just as unworthy individuals have held leadership positions in years past, today, in this 21st Century, we have a president who is ineffective and unworthy. We have a reference when we examine leaders from the Bible's Old Testament. Secondly, and extremely important is to recognize that it is the administrator who sets the tone for any institution. We see various types of leadership played throughout history. Effective leadership can present a picture of hope and persuade people to strive because of leadership! In the words of DL Hugley during his guest presence on the Bill Maher show, "Obama brought out the best of us. Donald Trump brought out the worst of us."

A historical perspective encompasses chapter two. One individual who best reflects the current leadership of the 45th president is Abimelech, son of Gideon. The Book of Judges, chapter nine, in the Holy Bible, illuminates his systematic actions to the detriment of many. The inclusion of Abimelech's immediate family reflects the family of the current president. As the precursor to present-day leadership in American politics, chapter three summarizes chapter nine of Judges and the events that led to the installation of Abimelech, the unworthy king. This chapter correlates the behaviors between Donald Trump and King Abimelech as articulated during November 6, 2016, Sunday morning sermon, "Living in tumbleweed times," by Rev. Dr. Ralph Douglas West. Chapter four takes an in-depth look at the manifestation of chapter nine in 21st Century politics. The underlings of Trump reflect the type of individuals like those solicited by Abimelech to execute an ungodly agenda. (For this document, Number 45 and Donald Trump are interchangeable.)

The Democratic Party and the previous presidential policies once established for the good of all Americans was systematically removed and or altered by the current president's agenda incorporates chapter five. Chapter six provides a reality check on the Trump cabinet. Chapter seven examines alternative facts. Kelly Ann Conway coined this phrase during an interview with Anderson Cooper of CNN and Chuck Todd of MSNBC. The Affordable Care Act, a tremendous contribution to the American quality of life, also encompasses chapter seven.

Sometimes we tend to forget the benefits of a worthy leader, like the children of Israel in the Old Testament. To help us remember, I present a comparison of what once was and what is now in chapter eight. An American reality check encompasses chapter nine. All the variables associated with the current political system encapsulates closing chapter ten. I include a message of thanks to my Pastor, Rev. Dr. Ralph Douglas West.

Actual statements incorporate much of the information in this document with extractions from news reports from MSNBC, CNN, New York Times, The Los Angeles Times, and websites. My commentary is limited as the reader unfamiliar with the Trump political climate and events would possibly find it difficult to believe the transition from a quasi-normal and acceptable America to a truly abnormal, attempted isolated, deprived, and dysfunctional American political system. This transition is based on the promise of Number 45 to make America great again. The question was, at whose expense and at what cost to all Americans?

CHAPTER TWO

Historical Perspective

Throughout history, countries have risen and fallen as a result of effective and ineffective leadership. European and Western historians will cite certain countries. Thousands of years before cities in Italy, and the European empires, Egyptian kings reigned supreme. The reign dates back well before the 12th century B.C. For example, King Taharqa, 690-664 BC, was known for his battles. Isaiah 37:9 and 2nd Kings 19:9 mentioned Taharqa as one who waged war against King Hezekiah. 13th Century, Mansa Musa, identified as the richest man in the world for all time, accumulated a fortune of 400 billion dollars from the production of ivory, salt, and gold. Queen Nefertiti, the female warrior, ruled with her husband, King Akhenaton, during the 15th Century of Egypt and continued ruling, after his death. King Hannibal is known for being a military strategist. History records his army infiltrating and conquering Italy-a country that is seen today as the bastion of the Catholic faith. King Nzenga Mvemba of the Kongo is known as the first Christian king in the Kongo. The contributions from African kings are visible on the walls in the Valley of the Kings in Egypt. The wall paintings portray stories of the rise and fall of kings and cultures and those who held leadership positions. The metaphysical and physical construction of sciences, cultures, scholarship, medicines, mathematics, and organizations to European countries can find its genesis in Egypt, Africa.

The National Interest (2017) selected five of what they considered the most significant empires on Earth over a five-thousand-year span. They cited the Achaemenid Persian Empire founded by Cyrus the Great around 550 BC.E., who went by the title of King of Kings (Shahanshah).

The Arab Empire, also known as the Caliphate, was a political entity founded by the Muslim Prophet Muhammad. His reign encompassed most of Arabia by the time of his death in 632 C.E. The Mongol Empire was another empire that originated on the periphery. They fought against and defeated enemies much more powerful and populous than themselves. It was the world's largest contiguous land empire, one that struck terror into all its enemies. The Mongol warlord Temujin assumed the title of Genghis Khan in 1206 C.E. Picking off parts of China as many previous stepped tribes had done, the Mongol Empire expanded. British institutions of representative democracy inspired French enlightenment philosophers such as Montesquieu to devise theories of government that influenced other European states.

Moving forward, Romulus, the last of the Roman emperors in the west, was overthrown by the Germanic leader Odoacer and became the first Barbarian to rule in Rome. European cultures reflect the year of 476 BC, C.E. The order that the Roman Empire had brought to Western Europe lasting for 1000 years was no more. Historians cite many reasons for the fall of kings that range from military losses, the invasion of Germanic countries to the rise of Christianity. For all these reasons, we can look at leadership.

Finally, we have the United States of America. The main characteristics are commitment to liberalism, the rule of law, civil rights, and trade that were inherited from the British and spread throughout the world. Sadly, America has had some presidents who contradicted the main characteristics of this country. RANKER (2017) Vote on Everything, an online website, identified Woodrow Wilson, Warren G. Harding, and Harry S. Truman at the top of the list. In the 1920s, Truman was encouraged to join the Ku Klux Klan to bolster his chances to win re-election for judge in Jackson County, Missouri. Rumor has it that Truman was a KKK member in name only and did not participate in any activities. Little has been acknowledged about Wilson's involvement in the group, but documents prove his membership. To add to this list would be Andrew Johnson, Lincoln's vice president infamously gained prominence for attempting to sabotage the efforts of Lincoln and opposing the 14th Amendment.

In contrast, America has had several outstanding presidents on the national and international stage. My favorites include John Adams, remembered for paying African Americans to work his farmland rather than owned slaves. Abraham Lincoln understood that America had entered the world stage after the Civil War and would not be viable with the existence of slavery. Franklin D. Roosevelt sought to establish social and humane programs. Rejected by American politics, European and Scandinavian countries implemented free health care, family medical leave, and the like. Lyndon B. Johnson, as a young senator, challenged the status quo regarding voting rights for African Americans. John F. Kennedy stepped out of his comfort zone to aggressively promote civil rights. Barack Obama understood the importance of maintaining the environment, health care, free education, and keeping a landmark business in America and established so much more for all Americans. I have selected these individuals as they exemplified a commitment to liberalism, the rule of law, civil rights, and trade. Historians have ranked Barack Obama the 12th best president of all time, the highest-rated since President Ronald Reagan, in a 2017 C-SPAN survey. Less than a month after exiting the White House, Obama received high marks from presidential historians for his pursuit of "equal justice for all" and for his commanding "moral authority," ranking third and seventh among all former presidents in each respective category. The 44th president also cracked a top 10 ranking for his "economic management" and public persuasion.

America, by and large, is a religious nation, meaning that there is a belief in a higher power. The Pew Research Center (2014) showed Christians encompassing 70.6% of the adult population; 46.5%

professed attendance at a variety of churches that could be considered Protestant, and 20.8% professed Roman Catholic beliefs. Since the publication of that data, there has been a drop in religious beliefs. For example, updated information on Pew Research-Religion and Public Life indicates that there is a drop of 92% to 89% among those who believe in God. As such, we can assume that the Bible is still used directly or indirectly as a guide for leadership. As such, the Biblical record of King Abimelech found in the Book of Judges Chapter Nine reflects an unworthy leader.

Summary of Judges 9: History of Abimelech

Judge Abimelech was the son of Gideon and ruler of the city of Shechem. Gideon, a Godly man of courage who was judge over Israel, had many wives that resulted in the birth of seventy sons. Abimelech was one of the sons of Jerubbaal, concubine from Shechem. The character of Abimelech indicates his ambition and desire was to rule over people. Judges 9:22 states that his determination resulted in a three-year reign as king over Israel but not as a king sanctioned by God. Israel had forgotten their God and the laws handed down by Moses.

Interestingly, supported by his mother and her clan Abimelech used strategies and tactics to become king. The Bible suggests that the succession for kingship placed his position in the family line at the lower end of the totem pole. Given this, Abimelech presented a question. "Do you think it would be good to have all seventy of Gideon's sons ruling us? Wouldn't you rather have just one man for the king?" Abimelech would make a good king, and he's related to us." On behalf of Abimelech, the request was introduced by his mother to the uncles. The leaders of Shechem were approached and agreed. "Yes." "It would be better for one of our relatives as the king." Abimelech is given seventy pieces of silver from the house of Baal-berith. He then used the silver to hire a gang of mercenaries who would do anything for money. To solidify his position, Abimelech, and his soldiers, went to his father's home in Ophrah and brought out Gideon's other sons to a large rock. With only Jotham, the youngest son who escaped, they were all murdered. The leaders of Shechem, including the priests and the military officers, met at the tree next to the sacred rock in Shechem to crown Abimelech king. After hearing of his brother's deaths, Jotham gave a speech from the top of Mount Gerizim in the form of a parable to the people of Shechem. In essence, Jotham uses an analogy of a tree to be king over Israel. He introduces the olive tree, with its extended branches and medicinal products. He moves on to the fig tree that produces liquid spirit-wine. Both respond, 'No.' The thorn bush was last to be asked to be king over Israel. This object produces nothing. It cannot provide shade, has no medicinal qualities, and cannot lend support to anything or anyone. However, the thorn bush agreed but warned that there would be consequences if it is not supported.

From that parable, Jotham reminded the residents how his father, Gideon, fought and rescued the people of Shechem from the Midianites. He also reminded the people that the reward for his father's effort was the killing of his brothers on a rock. Jotham asked, should Abimelech be king? He is from one of my father's slave girls. And was it right to make Abimelech your king? [Again] he's merely the son of my father's slave girl. Being a king was based on family. He did not have that characteristic necessary for an effective king. Jotham wished them well but also stated that if the kingship of Abimelech is wrong, then the people and the king would come to a tragic end. For safety from his brother, Jotham relocated to the town of Beer.

Abimelech Destroys Shechem

As I read that chapter, I found that what is not sanctioned by God is short-lived. And in the 23rd verse, God dispatched an evil spirit to the men of Shechem to deal treacherously with Abimelech. He turned the leaders of Shechem against Abimelech. God remembered the murdered sons of Gideon. Second, God's chosen people, the Israelites, appeared to have gotten amnesia. The exodus from Egypt, the parting of the Red Sea, provisions during the Israelites wilderness experience, and the laws laid down in the Ten Commandants were not even a distant memory. This point becomes a salient factor as the Bible clearly shows that God will use an unworthy leader to bring judgment on His people.

As people become disgruntled, plans for Abimelech's destruction are in play. Shechem residents work in concert and identify Gaad, son of Ebed, who stirred a rebellion against Abimelech. He, in turn, retaliated with a war on Shechem, then Thebez. For shelter against Abimelech and his army, the people fled to the strong tower located in the middle of the city and set themselves on the tower roof. As he seeks to set fire to the door, an unknown woman dropped a part of a millstone that landed on the head of Abimelech. Like King Saul in 2nd Samuel, Abimelech, a wounded king, asked to be killed by his armor-bearer. Given his character, I am sure he would not want to be killed by a woman. Judges 9:50-56 depicted these events in the Old Testament of the Bible.

Below are excerpts and a summary from *Living in tumbleweed times*.

There is no doubt that since the 2016 presidential election, many Americans are living under the umbrella of uncertainty based on the leadership. The first Sunday after the election, founder and Pastor Ralph Douglas West of the Church without Walls in Houston, Texas, presented a sermon on leadership. Centered on the story of Abimelech in the book of Judges, Chapter Nine, he has gained national attention from his message, Living in Tumble Weed Times. Not to reiterate the parable of Jotham and the trees, I would like to bring your attention to his reflection on leadership.

Bringing an understanding of leadership from the 19th through the 21st Century, Pastor West made one simple and powerful statement. Leadership matters. He recalled an example of a worthy president as Abraham Lincoln and Andrew Johnson an example of unworthy leadership. In big business, General Electric diminished after the retirement of Jack Welsh. Wendy's Hamburger's Dave Thomas came out of retirement to restore his company. The death of Steve Jobs appeared to bring about creativity concerns, even though Smartphones and iPhones continue to be enhanced. Leadership matters even in religious, communal life. We can look to the life and contributions of Rev. Dr. Martin Luther King, Jr., as leader of the Southern Christian Leadership Conference (SCLC). We find that charisma, and the ability to motivate many Americans, at times, cannot be replaced. Yet, there were worthy leaders like Ralph Abernathy and Joseph Lowery. The prominence held at one time in American history was no longer evident on a national scale.

Reverting to the Bible, Pastor West recalled the desire of the Israelites to have a king. The most well-known throughout the ages was King David, said to be the apple of God's eye and far more prominent than his predecessor, King Saul. Following was King Solomon, a man of wisdom but, like his father, suffered from human weaknesses. Unlike the heart of King David and the wisdom of King Solomon, the Israelites suffered under the leadership of King Rehoboam, who was considered undesirable.

He disregarded good advice. He adhered to ill advice. He was hot-headed, uncontrollable, easily agitated; he was one who had a bad temperament, poor pose, and posture under pressure. And, he did something that no one else in Israel history had ever done, and that was to divide the kingdoms. Anyone in that day and anyone who's a fan of history will tell you, leadership matters. "And where worthy leadership is absent, unworthy leadership will take its place." Certain aspects of the life and actions of Rehoboam and Abimelech are evidenced in the current leadership in America" (Pastor West).

History has shown that the door for leadership takes on many faces. One leadership opportunity may be willingly opened and accepted by a worthy leader. An individual is considered worthy of leadership and prepared. Yet, that person is not selected. A prepared leader may choose a different path. Edward the 8th, a British royalist, renounced his leadership position to marry an American divorcé. His brother, King George VI, who stuttered, was not prepared but accepted the role. The King Speech, an Oscar award movie, reflects his story. Finally, the door to leadership is opened, and the person walking through it may not be worthy.

Pastor West reminded us that our life in the 21st Century is unlike the kings and rulers of centuries or years past. We live in a democratic system of checks and balances. We have had worthy and unworthy leaders. We serve a God who is less interested in politics. God is far more interested in man's humanity, and the principles laid out in the Ten Commandments, and the fruits of the spirit articulated in the New Testament. These attributes incorporate common decency, common sense, love of fellow man and woman. When Godly characteristics are not visible, either directly or indirectly, "God can use what is under judgment to execute judgment upon God's own people" (Pastor West).

Reflecting on the president, Donald J. Trump, and the American political system, Pastor West reminds us, as Christians, it is a good time to be alive. We have hope and a future that is based on the Words of God, not on the person in the White House. The analogy of tumbleweed is played-out in the behavior of the current president. The following chapters provide an opportunity to examine the first six months of the American political system, presidential cabinet members' and visualizing the comparisons with Abimelech's ascension to leadership. Let's take a look down memory lane beginning with the first few months of the Trump administration.

CHAPTER THREE

Paying homage to the making of a dictator

Hail to the Chief! A peek at Number 45: The President's oval table;

EPA Administrator Scott Pruitt

"I actually arrived back this morning at 1 o'clock from Italy and the G-7 summit focused on the environment. And our message there was the United States is going to be focused on growth and protecting the environment. And it was received well." (…)

Defense Secretary James Mattis

"Mr. President, it's an honor to represent the men and women of the Department of Defense. And we are grateful for the sacrifices our people are making in order to strengthen our military, so our diplomats always negotiate from a position of strength. Thank you."(…)

Department of Homeland Security, Secretary John Kelly

"In the five months that I've been at the job, we have gone a long way to facilitate the -- improve the legal movement of people and commerce across our borders, yet at the same time, we have gone a long way to safeguarding our borders, particularly the southern border, working with all of our partners to the south." (…)

US Trade Representative Robert Lighthizer

"First of all, I apologize for being late to work. I got bogged down in that swamp that you've been trying to drain."(…) Secretary of State

Rex Tillerson: "Thank you for the honor to serve the country. It's a great privilege you've given me."

Small Business Administrator Linda McMahon

"I've been traveling around the country, and what I'm continuing to hear is this renewed optimism from small businesses." (…)

Director of National Intelligence, Dan Coat

"It's a joy to be working with the people that I have inherited, and we are going to provide -- continue to provide you with the very best intelligence we can, so you can formulate policies to deal with these issues." (…) Interior Secretary, Ryan Zinke

"Mr. President, as your SEAL on your staff … it's an honor to be your steward of our public lands and the generator of energy dominance. I am deeply honored."

Education Secretary Betsy DeVos

"It's a privilege to serve, to serve the students of this country, and to work to ensure that every child has an equal opportunity to get a great education, and therefore a great future."(…)

Commerce Secretary Wilbur Ross

"Mr. President, thank you for the opportunity to help fix the trade deficit and other things. The other countries are gradually getting used to the (inaudible) the free rides are somewhat over with. They're not happy with this, but I think (inaudible) growing recognition that (inaudible) have a chance to help you live up to your campaign promises." (…)

Energy Secretary, Rick Perry

"America is not stepping back but we're stepping into place and sending some messages; that we're still going to be leaders in the world when it comes to the climate, but we're not going to be held hostage to some executive order that was ill thought out. And so, my hat's off to you for taking that stance and presenting a clear message around the world that America's going to continue to lead in the area of energy."

Housing and Urban Development Secretary, Ben Carson

"Mr. President, it's been a great honor to -- to work with you. Thank you for your strong support of HUD and for all the others around this table that I've worked with."

Reminder: Donald Trump once compared Ben Carson's "pathology" to a child molester.

Labor Secretary Alexander Acosta:

"I am privileged to be here. Deeply honored, and I want to thank you for being -- your commitment to the American workers." (…)

Veterans Affairs Secretary David Shulkin:

"Mr. President, thank you for your support and commitment to honoring our responsibility to America's veterans. I know that this is personally very important to you." (…)

UN Ambassador, Nikki Haley:

"It's a new day at the United Nations. You know, we now have a very strong voice. People know what the United States is for, they know what we're against, and they see us leading across the board. And so, I think the international community knows we're back." (…)

Treasury Secretary, Steve Mnuchin, "It was a great honor traveling with you around the country for the last year and an even greater honor to be here serving on your Cabinet." (…)

CIA Director Mike Pompeo,

"Mr. President, it's an honor to serve as your CIA director. It's an incredible privilege to lead the men and women who are providing intelligence so that we can do the national security mission. And, in the finest traditions of the CIA, I'm not going to share a damn thing in front of the media." (...)

Transportation Secretary Elaine Chao,

"Mr. President, last week was a great (inaudible). It was infrastructure week. Thank you so much for coming over to the Department of Transportation. Hundreds and hundreds of people were just so thrilled, hanging out, watching (inaudible) ceremony." (...)

Attorney General Jeff Sessions:

"We are receiving, as you know -- I'm not sure the rest of you fully understand -- the support of law enforcement all over America. They have been very frustrated. They are so thrilled that we have a new idea that we're going to support them and work together too, properly, lawfully fight the rising crime that we are seeing.... The response is fabulous around the country." (...)

Office of Management and Budget Director Mick Mulvaney:

"Thanks for the kind words about the budget. You're absolutely right: We are going to be able to take care of the people who really need it. And at the same time, with your direction, we were able to also focus on the forgotten man and woman who are the folks who are paying those taxes." (...) Agriculture Secretary Sonny Perdue:

"I want to congratulate you on the men and women you've placed around this table.... This is the team you've assembled that's working hand in glove with -- for the men and women of America, and I want to -- I want to thank you for that. These are -- are great team members and we're on your team."

Health and Human Services Secretary Tom Price:

"Mr. President, what an incredible honor it is to lead the Department of Health and Human Services at this pivotal time under your leadership. I can't thank you enough for the privileges you've given me and the leadership that you've shown. It seems like there's an international flair to the messages that are being delivered. I had the opportunity to represent the United States at the G-20 Health Summit in Berlin and at the World Health Assembly in Geneva. And I can't tell you how excited and enthusiastic folks are about the United States leadership as it relates to global health security." (…)

Vice President Mike Pence

"It is just the greatest privilege of my life is to serve as the -- as vice president to the President who's keeping his word to the American people and assembling a team that's bringing real change, real prosperity, real strength back to our nation."

They kissed the wanna-be king's ring. What have they done? And where are they now?

CHAPTER FOUR

Number 45 Religious Cabinet

Isaiah 10 (1-3)
"Woe to those who make unjust laws, to those who issue oppressive
decrees, (2) to deprive the poor of their rights and withhold justice
from the oppressed of my people, making widows their prey and
robbing the fatherless. (3) What will you do on the day of reckoning,
when disaster comes from afar? To whom will you run for help?
Where will you leave your riches? (New International Version.)"

The need for being a practicing Christian, a leader who has a
personal relationship with God is essential, particularly in government.
Elected officials set laws, policies, and programs that affect millions
of Americans. Given this fact, these individuals need to demonstrate
morals, ethics, human decency, and a love for all humankind.

According to an analysis by Pew Research Center (2017), nearly 91
percent of the 115th Congress is Christian. That's significantly higher
than the 75% of American adults who identify as Christian and just
slightly less than the 95% of Congress members who identified as
Christian in 1961. A whopping 99% of Republicans in the House and
Senate – all but two – are Christian. Eighty percent of Democrats in
Congress are Christian. And, apart from Jewish Republicans, Lee Zeldin
of New York and David Kustoff of Tennessee, all other non-Christian
members of Congress are Democrats, including newly elected Hindu
representatives Ro Khanna, D-California, and Raja Krishnamoorthi,

D-Illinois. The 115th Congress's freshman class also includes five new Jewish members and Buddhist Rep. Colleen Hanabusa, D-Hawaii.

The Head Heart Hand Blog (2017), produced by David Murray, showed the number of Christians in Number 45's cabinet. Mike Pence (Vice-president), "My Christian faith is at the heart of who I am" and "I'm a Christian, a conservative and a Republican, in that order."

Reince Priebus (previous Chief of Staff), at the writing of this document, was found to be a longtime member of the Greek Orthodox Church. "At Grace Church, he is known as a principled, devout Christian."

Jeff Sessions (Attorney General-removed): According to an earlier Senate bio, he "has served as a lay leader and as a Sunday school teacher at his family's church, Ashland Place United Methodist Church, in Mobile, Alabama. He served as the Chairman of his church's Administrative Board and chosen as a delegate to the annual Alabama Methodist Conference."

Dr. Ben Carson (Secretary of Housing and Urban Development) interview with Christianity Today stated. "I would describe myself, first of all as a Christian. Evangelical in the sense that I believe we have a responsibility to proclaim the gospel and show other people why we live the way that we do, and hopefully that will affect their lives. I think that's a very important component of what we do."

Betsy DeVos (Secretary of Education) has "deep ties to the Christian Reformed community," and "heavily influenced by Abraham Kuyper." She sees education as "one of the ways that God advances his kingdom."

Rex Tillerson was Secretary of State. According to Religious News Service (2016), he and his wife donated $5,000-$10,000 to the National Association of Congregational Christian Churches in 2012. He was reported to be a devout Christian who attends church weekly and teaches Bible Study.

Scott Pruitt was removed as Secretary of the EPA-Environmental Protection Agency. According to the Oklahoma Office of Attorney General, the Pruitts are members of the First Baptist Church of Broken Arrow where Pruitt serves as a deacon.

Mike Pompeo (Central Intelligence Agency-CIA) and his family attend East Minster Presbyterian Church, where he serves as a deacon and teaches Sunday School to fifth - graders.

Nikki Haley was United Nations Ambassador. She is commented in Christianity Today magazine. "My faith in Christ has a profound impact on my daily life, and I look to Him for guidance with every decision I make." In an interview, she said: "God has blessed my family in so many ways, and my faith in the Lord gives me great strength daily. Being a Christian is not about words, but about living for Christ every day."

Other publications provide additional information. The Religion News Service (12/13/201) article: Cabinet: Trump Advisors: The Faith Factor, identified the religious affiliation of several Cabinet members. Tom Price is a member of the United Methodist Church and considers himself to be a conservative Christian. Steve Bannon, at the time of this writing, is shown as not having any religious affiliation.

The extent of individuals who are Christians in the Number 45 cabinet or who are willing to share their religious beliefs and affiliations is limited. There also appears to be a contradiction between what is believed and what is accomplished.

Presidential Cabinet Members: A Reality Check

I cannot help but reflect upon Judges 9. Abimelech was given 70 coins and hired the most terrible individuals to do his bidding. Number 45 was given a salary and appointed some extremely questionable individuals to "Make his America great again." That was the campaign message promoted by Number 45. The translation is to resurrect the tangible acts of racism that were prevalent before the Civil Rights Movement. This was evident during his campaign and since being in the White House. Unfortunately, on Friday, August 11, and 12, 2017, the world witnessed the first aggressive public large-scale phase of racism from Trump supporters. Hundreds of white males and some females carrying Tekke torches converged on Charlottesville, Virginia, in response to the removal of a Confederate statue. The march was said to be peaceful. In actuality, marchers came with sticks. Some had guns and wearing military garb. The impact of racist ideology resulted in the death of a young white woman walking in opposition to the Klan and its followers. Making matters even worse, Number 45, publicly stated that, in essence, that he supported the behavior Nazi and KKK groups. During a Tuesday, August 15, 2017, press conference. Excerpts of his responses are as follows:

Trump: "As I said — remember this, Saturday — we condemn in the strongest possible terms this egregious display of hatred, bigotry, and violence. It has no place in America, and then I went on from there. Now, here's the thing. Excuse me, excuse me. Take it nice and easy. Here's the thing. When I make a statement, I like to be correct. I want the facts. This event just happened. A lot of the event didn't even happen yet, as we were speaking. This event just happened. Before I make a statement, I need the facts, so I don't want to rush into a statement. (…) And honestly, if the press were not fake and if it was honest, the press would have said what I said was very nice. But unlike you and unlike — excuse me — unlike you and unlike the media, before I make a statement, I like to know the facts. (…)"

Reporter: The CEO of Wal-Mart said you missed a critical opportunity to help bring the country together. Did you?

Trump: "Not at all. I think the country — look, you take a look. I've created over a million jobs since I'm president. The country is booming, the stock market is setting records. We have the highest employment numbers we've ever had in the history of our country. We're doing record business. We have the highest levels of enthusiasm. So, the head of Wal-Mart, whom I know, who is a very nice guy, was making a political statement. I mean, I do it the same way. You know why? Because I want to make sure, when I make a statement that the statement is correct, and there was no way — there was no way of making a correct statement that early. I had to see the facts, unlike a lot of reporters — unlike a lot of reporters. I know, David Duke (a previous leader and supporter of the KKK) was there. I wanted to see the facts, and the facts as they started coming out were very well-stated. In fact, everybody said his statement was beautiful. If he would have made it sooner, that would have been good. I couldn't have made it sooner because I didn't know all of the facts. Frankly, people still don't know all of the facts. It was very important — excuse me, excuse me. It was very important to me to get the facts out and correctly, because if I would have made a fast statement — and the first statement was made without knowing much other than what we were seeing. The second statement was made with knowledge, with great knowledge. There are still things — excuse me, there are still things that people don't know. I want to make a statement with knowledge. I wanted to know the facts. Okay."

Concerning Steve Bannon, founder of Alt-Right organization;

Reporter: Two questions. Was this terrorism, and can you tell us how you're feeling about your chief strategist Steve Bannon?

Trump: "Well, I think the driver of the car is a disgrace to himself, his family, and this country, and that is ... you can call it terrorism. You can call it murder. You can call it whatever you want. I would just call it the fastest one to come up with a good verdict. That's what I'd call it. Because there is a question. Is it murder? Is it terrorism? And then you get into legal semantics. The driver of the car is a murderer and what he did was a horrible, horrible inexcusable thing."

Trump: "Well, we'll see. Look, I like Mr. Bannon, he's a friend of mine, but Mr. Bannon came on very late — you know that. I went through 17 senators; governors and I won all the primaries. Mr. Bannon came on very much later than that, and I like him, he's a good man. He is not a racist, I can tell you that. He's a good person, he actually, gets a very unfair press in that regard. But we'll see what happens with Mr. Bannon, but he's a good person and I think the press treats him frankly very unfairly."

Trump: "Those people were also there because they wanted to protest the taking down of a statue of Robert E. Lee. So … Excuse me. And you take a look at some of the groups and you see, and you'd know it if you were honest reporters — which in many cases you're not. But many of those people were there to protest the taking down of the statue of Robert E. Lee. So, this week it's Robert E. Lee. I noticed that Stonewall Jackson is coming down. I wonder is it George Washington next week and is it, Thomas Jefferson, the week after? You know, you really do have to ask yourself, where does it stop? But they were there to protest- excuse me. You take a look the night before, they were there to protest the taking down of the statue of Robert E. Lee. Infrastructure question. Go ahead."

Trump: "No. No. There were people in that rally — and I looked the night before. If you look, people were protesting very quietly the taking down of the statue of Robert E. Lee. I'm sure in that group there were some bad ones. The following day it looked like they had some rough, bad people: neo-Nazis, white nationalists, whatever you want to call them. But you had a lot of people in that group that was there to innocently protest — and very legally protest because you know- I don't know if you know, they had a permit. The other group didn't have a permit. So, I only tell you this. There are two sides to a story. I thought what took place was a horrible moment for our country, a horrible moment. But there are two sides to the country.

Does anybody have a final- does anybody- you have an infrastructure question?"

To ensure that racist acts are permissible, he appointed Jeff Session. Michelle Ye Hee Lee (December 2, 2016) wrote in The Fact Checker "Senator Sessions was denied appointment as a federal judge in 1986 for a slew of racist comments including calling the work of the NAACP and ACLU as 'un-American.' He has also repeatedly spoken out against the federal Voting Rights Act."

NAACP statement on November 18, 2016, Session's rejection was based on his comments on race and his role in prosecuting a voter fraud case against Black civil rights activists in Alabama. (…) The testimony came from former assistant U.S. Attorney Thomas Figures, the only Black Assistant U.S. Attorney in Alabama at the time. Mr. Figures died in January 2015.

It is diabolical how some African Americans are used by a well-known racist who wants to be respected as a person who embraces all Americans. During his confirmation hearing, Session introduced two Black males who regarded Secretary Session as such a great guy.

Rick Perry is documented in the Washington Post (June 2015) that the killing of nine African Americans in a church during a Wednesday night Bible Study class was an 'accident'. He was also recorded as saying, "This is the MO (modus operation) of this administration (President Obama administration). Secretary Perry continued, "Anytime there is an accident like this the president is clear: he doesn't like for Americans to have guns, and so he uses every opportunity. This is another one to basically go parrot that message."

Ousted Past Secretary Pruitt, in past years, had sued the Environmental Protection Agency. He set out to undo some and dismantle other sections of that agency, making it ineffective. Could this be the fox guarding the henhouse? Absolutely! Scientists from all over the globe had formed a pact to address global warming. His concern about this planet meant nothing. I am convinced that his interest was how much money he can make.

Secretary DeVos was so unpopular with educational initiatives that she had to be escorted by bodyguards. Picket signs against her public-school policies were nearly nation-wide. At the time of this writing, she was being sued by eighteen states for removing funds from public schools and placing it in charter schools. I wonder how much it cost her to sit at the Oval table in the White House?

Valerie Strauss (December 8, 2016) article found in Andrew Harrer of Bloomberg News wrote: "President-elect Donald Trump has made a number of controversial cabinet nominations already. But none seems more inappropriate, or more contrary to reason, than his choice of DeVos to lead the Department of Education. DeVos isn't an educator, or an education leader. She's not an expert in pedagogy or curriculum or school governance. In fact, she has no relevant credentials or experience for a job setting standards, and guiding dollars for the nation's public schools. She is in essence a lobbyist. Someone who has used extraordinary wealth to influence the conversation about education reform, and to bend that conversation to her ideological convictions despite the dearth of evidence supporting them."

Budget Director, Secretary Mulvaney visited the MSNBC, Morning Joe Show early in his appointment. He cannot see the benefit of Meals on Wheels, and diabetes's caused their problem. "They, themselves are the main reason for their illness."

Secretary Tillerson, in a Politico Magazine, June 2017, headline, Present at the Destruction: How Rex Tillerson is destroying the State Department. The article stated, "What we now know is that the building is being run by a tiny clique of ideologues who know nothing about the department but have insulated themselves from the people who do."

"Tillerson and his isolated and inexperienced cadres are going about reorganizing the department based on little more than gut feeling. They are going about it with vigor. And there is little Congress can seemingly do, though lawmakers control the purse strings. It's hard to stop an agency from destroying itself." "(...) Perhaps Tillerson as a D.C. and foreign policy novice is simply being a good soldier, following through on edicts from White House ideologues like Steve Bannon. Perhaps he thinks he is running the State like a business. (...)."

Vice President Mike Pence refused to pardon a wrongly imprisoned African American man. The Daily Beast (2/15/17), Keith Cooper, was sentenced to 40 years in prison for a violent robbery he did not commit. Using DNA, the prosecutor found him innocent. He was released and sought a pardon to have his record expunged. Pence, as governor, refused to grant Mr. Cooper's petition. Even his prosecutor came to agree Cooper was innocent. It took a new governor to clear his name.

Dr. Carol Paris, psychiatrist and president of Physicians for a National Health Program (PNHP), (January 2017) described in Common Dreams publication, Tom Price, Secretary of Health and Human Services, has extensive documentation for being pro-big-business, and a proponent of dismantling Medicare. Paul Ryan, Speaker of the House and Price, sought to allocate funds to seniors, have them purchase a voucher, and purchase their medical insurance from a private insurance market. In essence, seniors would pay for a service previously paid.

Michael Brune (September 19, 2017), Executive Director of the Sierra Club, wrote in the Sierra Club Newsletter. Interior Secretary Zinke's recommendations were to strip ten national monuments from critical protections. Brune pointed out the effort was to expose sacred lands to drilling, mining, and logging, and the disasters that will follow. He cites Cascade-Siskiyou National Monument, Oregon; Gold Butte National Monument, Nevada; Organ Mountains-Desert Peaks National Monument, New Mexico. Rio Grande del Norte National Monument,

New Mexico; Northeast Canyons and Seamounts, Atlantic Ocean; Pacific Remote Islands National Monument, Pacific Ocean; Rose Atoll National Monument, Pacific Ocean; Katahdin Woods and Waters; Bears Ears, and Grand Staircase-Escalante. According to Brune, the purpose was for "fossil fuel development on and around the public lands."

It appears that none of those individuals understood ethics or morals. It also appeared that common sense is not in their repertoire of humanity. What is remarkable are those individuals who had lost their sense of reasoning. The analogy of tumbleweed is reflective of those who appear to have lost their moral compass. Judges, chapter nine, tells us that God sometimes brings judgment on His nation. The judgment is upon the people who would select an unworthy leader in the first place.

CHAPTER FIVE

Alternative facts

Alternative facts appear to suggest that like father, and like son extends to the wife also

So, this is America's White House? According to David Leonhardt and Stuart A. Thompson of the New York Times, Number 45 has given fabrications- lies most of the days he has been in the White House. They cite the following dates and statements:

Jan. 21 "I wasn't a fan of Iraq. I didn't want to go into Iraq." (He was for an invasion before he was against it.)

Jan. 21 "A reporter for Time magazine — and I have been on their cover 14 or 15 times. I think we have the all-time record in the history of Time magazine." (Trump was on the cover 11 times and Nixon appeared 55 times.)

Jan. 23 "Between 3 million and 5 million illegal votes caused me to lose the popular vote." (There's no evidence of illegal voting.)

Jan. 25 "Now, the audience was the biggest ever. But this crowd was massive. Look how far back it goes. This crowd was massive." (Official aerial photos show Obama's 2009 inauguration was much more heavily attended.)

Jan. 25 "Take a look at the Pew reports (which show voter fraud.)" (The report never mentioned voter fraud.)

Jan. 25 "You had millions of people that now aren't insured anymore." (The real number is less than 1 million, according to the Urban Institute.)

Jan. 25 "So, look, when President Obama was there two weeks ago making a speech, very nice speech. Two people were shot and killed during his speech. You can't have that." (There were no gun homicide victims in Chicago that day.)

Jan. 26 "We've taken in tens of thousands of people. We know nothing about them. They can say they vet them. They didn't vet them. They have no papers. How can you vet somebody when you don't know anything about them, and you have no papers? How do you vet them? You can't." (Vetting lasts up to two years.)

Jan. 26 "I cut off hundreds of millions of dollars off one particular plane, hundreds of millions of dollars in a short period of time. It wasn't like I spent, like, weeks, hours, less than hours, and many, many hundreds of millions of dollars. And the plane's going to be better." (Most of the cuts were already planned.)

Jan. 28 "The coverage about me in the NY Times and the Washington Post has been so false and angry that the Times actually apologized to its dwindling subscribers and readers." (It never apologized.)

Jan. 29 "The Cuban-Americans, I got 84 percent of that vote." (There is no support for this.)

Jan. 30 "Only 109 people out of 325,000 were detained and held for questioning. Big problems at airports were caused by Delta computer outage." (At least 746 people were detained and processed, and the Delta outage happened two days later.)

Feb. 3 "Professional anarchists, thugs and paid protesters are proving the point of the millions of people who voted to Make America Great Again!" (There is no evidence of paid protesters.)

Feb. 4 "After being forced to apologize for its bad and inaccurate coverage of me after winning the election, the fake news NY Times is still lost!" (It never apologized.)

Feb. 5 "We had 109 people out of hundreds of thousands of travelers and all we did was vet those people very, very carefully." (About 60,000 people were affected.)

Feb. 6 "I have already saved more than $700 million when I got involved in the negotiation on the F-35." (Much of the price drop was projected before Trump took office.)

Feb. 6 "It's gotten to a point where it is not even being reported. And in many cases, the very, very dishonest press doesn't want to report it." (Terrorism has been reported on, often in detail.)

Feb. 6 "The failing @nytimes was forced to apologize to its subscribers for the poor reporting it did on my election win. Now they are worse!" (It didn't apologize.)

Feb. 6 "And the previous administration allowed it to happen because we shouldn't have been in Iraq, but we shouldn't have gotten out the way we got out. It created a vacuum, ISIS was formed." (The group's origins date to 2004.)

Feb. 7 "And yet the murder rate in our country is the highest it's been in 47 years, right? Did you know that? Forty-seven years." (It was higher in the 1980s and '90s.)

Feb. 7 "I saved more than $600 million. I got involved in negotiation on a fighter jet, the F-35." (The Defense Department projected this price drop before Trump took office.)

Feb. 9 "Chris Cuomo, in his interview with Sen. Blumenthal, never asked him about his long-term lie about his brave 'service' in Vietnam. Fake News!" (It was part of Cuomo's first question.)

Feb. 9 Sen. Richard Blumenthal "now misrepresents what Judge Gorsuch told him?" (The Gorsuch comments were later corroborated.)

Feb. 10 "I don't know about it. I haven't seen it. What report is that?" (Trump knew about Flynn's actions for weeks.)

Feb. 12 "Just leaving Florida. Big crowds of enthusiastic supporters lining the road that the Fake News media refuses to mention. Very dishonest!" (The media did cover it.)

Feb. 16 "We got 306 because people came out and voted like they've never seen before so that's the way it goes. I guess it was the biggest Electoral College win since Ronald Reagan." (George H.W. Bush, Bill Clinton and Barack Obama all won bigger margins in the Electoral College.)

Feb. 16 "That's the other thing that was wrong with the travel ban. You had Delta with a massive problem with their computer system at the airports." (Delta's problems happened two days later.)

Feb. 16 "Walmart announced it will create 10,000 jobs in the United States just this year because of our various plans and initiatives." (The jobs are a result of its investment plans announced in October 2016.)

Feb. 16 "When WikiLeaks, which I had nothing to do with, comes out and happens to give, they're not giving classified information." (Not always. They have released classified information in the past.)

Feb. 16 "We had a very smooth rollout of the travel ban. But we had a bad court. Got a bad decision." (The rollout was chaotic.)

Feb. 16 "They're giving stuff — what was said at an office about Hillary cheating on the debates. Which, by the way, nobody mentions. Nobody mentions that Hillary received the questions to the debates." (It was widely covered.)

Feb. 18 "And there was no way to vet those people. There was no documentation. There was no nothing." (Refugees receive multiple background checks, taking up to two years.)

Feb. 18 "You look at what's happening in Germany, you look at what's happening last night in Sweden. Sweden, who would believe this?" (Trump implied there was a terror attack in Sweden, but there was no such attack.)

Feb. 24 "By the way, you folks are in here — this place is packed, there are lines that go back six blocks." (There was no evidence of long lines.)

Feb. 24 "ICE came and endorsed me." (Only its union did.)

Feb. 24 "Obamacare covers very few people — and remember, deduct from the number all of the people that had great health care that they loved that was taken away from them — it was taken away from them." (Obamacare increased coverage by a net of about 20 million.)

Feb. 27 "Since Obamacare went into effect, nearly half of the insurers are stopped and have stopped from participating in the Obamacare exchanges." (Many fewer pulled out.)

Feb. 27 "On one plane, on a small order of one plane, I saved $725 million. And I would say I devoted about, if I added it up, all those calls, probably about an hour. So, I think that might be my highest and best use." (Much of the price cut was already projected.)

Feb. 28 "And now, based on our very strong and frank discussions, they are beginning to do just that." (NATO countries agreed to meet defense spending requirements in 2014.)

Feb. 28 "The E.P.A.'s regulators were putting people out of jobs by the hundreds of thousands." (There's no evidence that the Waters of the United States rule caused severe job losses.)

Feb. 28 "We have begun to drain the swamp of government corruption by imposing a five-year ban on lobbying by executive branch officials." (They can't lobby their former agency but can still become lobbyists.)

March 3 "It is so pathetic that the Dems have still not approved my full Cabinet." (Paperwork for the last two candidates was still not submitted to the Senate.)

March 4 "Terrible! Just found out that Obama had my 'wires tapped' in Trump Tower just before the victory. Nothing found. This is McCarthyism!" (There's no evidence of a wiretap.)

March 4 "How low has President Obama gone to tap my phones during the very sacred election process. This is Nixon/Watergate. Bad (or sick) guy!" (There's no evidence of a wiretap.)

March 7 "122 vicious prisoners, released by the Obama Administration from Gitmo, have returned to the battlefield. Just another terrible decision!" (113 of them were released by President George W. Bush.)

March 13 "I saved a lot of money on those jets, didn't I? Did I do a good job? More than $725 million on them." (Much of the cost cuts were planned before Trump.)

March 13 "First of all, it covers very few people." (About 20 million people gained insurance under Obamacare.)

March 15 "On the airplanes, I saved $725 million. Probably took me a half an hour if you added up all of the times." (Much of the cost cuts were planned before Trump.)

March 17 "I was in Tennessee — I was just telling the folks — and half of the state has no insurance company, and the other half is going to lose the insurance company." (There's at least one insurer in every Tennessee County.)

March 20 "With just one negotiation on one set of airplanes, I saved the taxpayers of our country over $700 million." (Much of the cost cuts were planned before Trump.)

March 21 "To save taxpayer dollars, I've already begun negotiating better contracts for the federal government — saving over $700 million on just one set of airplanes of which there are many sets." (Much of the cost cuts were planned before Trump.)

March 22 "I make the statement, everyone goes crazy. The next day they have a massive riot, and death, and problems." (Riots in Sweden broke out two days later and there were no deaths.)

March 22 "NATO, obsolete, because it doesn't cover terrorism. They fixed that." (It has fought terrorism since the 1980s.)

March 22 "Well, now, if you take a look at the votes, when I say that, I mean mostly they register wrong — in other words, for the votes, they register incorrectly and/or illegally. And they then vote. You have tremendous numbers of people." (There's no evidence of widespread voter fraud.)

March 29 "Remember when the failing @nytimes apologized to its subscribers, right after the election, because their coverage was so wrong. Now worse!" (It didn't apologize.)

March 31 "We have a lot of plants going up now in Michigan that were never going to be there if I — if I didn't win this election, those plants would never even think about going back. They were gone." (These investments were already planned.)

April 2 "And I was totally opposed to the war in the Middle East which I think finally has been proven, people tried very hard to say I wasn't, but you've seen that it is now improving." (He was for an invasion before he was against it.)

April 2 "Now, my last tweet — you know, the one that you are talking about, perhaps — was the one about being, in quotes, wiretapped, meaning surveilled. Guess what, it is turning out to be true." (There is still no evidence.)

April 5 "You have many states coming up where they're going to have no insurance company. O.K.? It's already happened in Tennessee. It's happening in Kentucky. Tennessee only has half coverage. Half the state is gone. They left." (Every marketplace region in Tennessee had at least one insurer.)

April 6 "If you look at the kind of cost-cutting we've been able to achieve with the military and at the same time ordering vast amounts of equipment — saved hundreds of millions of dollars on airplanes, and really billions, because if you take that out over a period of years it's many billions of dollars — I think we've had a tremendous success." (Much of the price cuts were already projected.)

April 11 "I like Steve, but you have to remember he was not involved in my campaign until very late. I had already beaten all the senators and all the governors, and I didn't know Steve." (He knew Steve Bannon since 2011.)

April 12 "You can't do it faster, because they're obstructing. They're obstructionists. So, I have people — hundreds of people that we're trying to get through. I mean you have — you see the backlog. We can't get them through." (At this point, he had not nominated anyone for hundreds of positions.)

April 12 "The New York Times said the word wiretapped in the headline of the first edition. Then they took it out of there fast when they realized." (There were separate headlines for print and web, but neither were altered.)

April 12 "The secretary general and I had a productive discussion about what more NATO can do in the fight against terrorism. I complained about that a long time ago and they made a change, and now they do fight terrorism." (NATO has been engaged in counterterrorism efforts since the 1980s.)

April 12 "Mosul was supposed to last for a week and now they've been fighting it for many months and so many more people died." (The campaign was expected to take months.)

April 16 "Someone should look into who paid for the small organized rallies yesterday. The election is over!" (There's no evidence of paid protesters.)

April 18 "The fake media goes, 'Donald Trump changed his stance on China.' I haven't changed my stance." (He did.)

April 21 "On 90 planes I saved $725 million. It's actually a little bit more than that, but it's $725 million." (Much of the price cuts were already projected.)

April 21 "When WikiLeaks came out ... never heard of WikiLeaks, never heard of it." (He criticized it as early as 2010.)

April 27 "I want to help our miners while the Democrats are blocking their healthcare." (The bill to extend health benefits for certain coal miners was introduced by a Democrat and was co-sponsored by mostly Democrats.)

April 28 "The trade deficit with Mexico is close to $70 billion, even with Canada its $17 billion trade deficit with Canada." (The U.S. had an $8.1 billion trade surplus, not deficit, with Canada in 2016.)

April 28 "She's running against someone who's going to raise your taxes to the sky, destroy your health care, and he's for open borders — lots of crime." (Those are not Jon Ossoff's positions.)

April 28 "The F-35 fighter jet program — it was way over budget. I've saved $725 million plus, just by getting involved in the negotiation." (Much of the price cuts were planned before Trump.)

April 29 "They're incompetent, dishonest people who after an election had to apologize because they covered it, us, me, but all of us, they covered it so badly that they felt they were forced to apologize because their predictions were so bad." (The Times did not apologize.)

April 29 "As you know, I've been a big critic of China, and I've been talking about currency manipulation for a long time. But I have to tell you that during the election, number one, they stopped." (China stopped years ago.)

April 29 "I've already saved more than $725 million on a simple order of F-35 planes. I got involved in the negotiation." (Much of the price cuts were planned before Trump.)

April 29 "We're also getting NATO countries to finally step up and contribute their fair share. They've begun to increase their contributions by billions of dollars, but we are not going to be satisfied until everyone pays what they owe." (The deal was struck in 2014.)

April 29 "When they talk about currency manipulation, and I did say I would call China, if they were, a currency manipulator, early in my tenure. And then I get there. Number one, they — as soon as I got elected, they stopped." (China stopped in 2014.)

April 29 "I was negotiating to reduce the price of the big fighter jet contract, the F-35, which was totally out of control. I will save billions and billions and billions of dollars." (Most of the cuts were planned before Trump.)

April 29 "I think our side's been proven very strongly. And everybody's talking about it." (There are still no evidence Trump's phones were tapped.)

May 1 "Well, we are protecting pre-existing conditions. And it'll be every good — bit as good on pre-existing conditions as Obamacare." (The bill weakens protections for people with pre-existing conditions.)

May 1 "The F-35 fighter jet — I saved — I got involved in the negotiation. Its 2,500 jets. I negotiated for 90 planes, lot 10. I got $725 million off the price." (Much of the price cuts were planned before Trump.)

May 1 "First of all, since I started running, they haven't increased their — you know, they have not manipulated their currency. I think that was out of respect to me and the campaign." (China stopped years ago.)

May 2 "I love buying those planes at a reduced price. I have been really — I have cut billions — I have to tell you this, and they can check, right, Martha? I have cut billions and billions of dollars off plane contracts sitting here." (Much of the cost cuts were planned before Trump.)

May 4 "Number two, they're actually not a currency [manipulator]. You know, since I've been talking about currency manipulation with respect to them and other countries, they stopped." (China stopped years ago.)

May 4 "We're the highest-taxed nation in the world." (We're not.)

May 4 "Nobody cares about my tax return except for the reporters." (Polls show most Americans do care.)

May 8 "You know we've gotten billions of dollars more in NATO than we're getting. All because of me." (The deal was struck in 2014.)

May 8 "But when I did his show, which by the way was very highly rated. It was high — highest rating. The highest rating he's ever had." (Colbert's "Late Show" debut had nearly two million more viewers.)

May 8 "Director Clapper reiterated what everybody, including the fake media already knows — there is 'no evidence' of collusion w/ Russia and Trump." (Clapper only said he wasn't aware of an investigation.)

May 12 "Again, the story that there was collusion between the Russians & Trump campaign was fabricated by Dems as an excuse for losing the election." (The F.B.I. was investigating before the election.)

May 12 "When James Clapper himself, and virtually everyone else with knowledge of the witch hunt, says there is no collusion, when does it end?" (Clapper said he wouldn't have been told of an investigation into collusion.)

May 13 "I'm cutting the price of airplanes with Lockheed." (The cost cuts were planned before he became president.)

May 26 "Just arrived in Italy for the G7. Trip has been very successful. We made and saved the USA many billions of dollars and millions of jobs." (He's referencing an arm deal that's not enacted and other apparent deals that weren't announced on the trip.)

June 1 "China will be allowed to build hundreds of additional coal plants. So, we can't build the plants, but they can, according to this agreement. India will be allowed to double its coal production by 2020." (The agreement doesn't allow or disallow building coal plants.)

June 1 "I've just returned from a trip overseas where we concluded nearly $350 billion of military and economic development for the United States, creating hundreds of thousands of jobs." (Trump's figures are inflated and premature.)

June 4 "At least 7 dead and 48 wounded in terror attack and Mayor of London says there is 'no reason to be alarmed!'" (The mayor was specifically talking about the enlarged police presence on the streets.)

June 5 "The Justice Dept. should have stayed with the original Travel Ban, not the watered down, politically correct version they submitted to S.C." (Trump signed this version of the travel ban, not the Justice Department.)

June 21 "They all say it's 'nonbinding.' Like hell it's nonbinding." (The Paris climate agreement is nonbinding — and Trump said so in his speech announcing the withdrawal.)

June 21 "Right now, we are one of the highest-taxed nations in the world." (We're not.)

The so called 'fake news' of CNN showed a side-by-side depiction of both speeches from Mrs. Obama and Mrs. Trump. During an interview on Airforce One, she was asked if she had written her speech during the presidential campaign. She responded, "Yes. I wrote my speech."

Mrs. Trump said: "*My parents impressed on me the values that you work hard for what you want in life; that your word is your bond and you do what you say and keep your promise; that you treat people with respect.*"

Mrs. Obama's speech in 2008 carried the lines: "*And Barack and I were raised with so many of the same values: that you work hard for what you want in life; that your word is your bond and you do what you say you're going to do; that you treat people with dignity and respect, even if you don't know them, and even if you don't agree with them.*"

Mrs. Trump's speech continued: "*[My parents] taught me to show the values and morals in my daily life. That is the lesson that I continue to pass along to our son. And we need to pass those lessons on to the many generations to follow because we want our children in this nation to know that the only limit to your achievements is the strength of your dreams and your willingness to work for them.*"

Mrs. Obama said: "*And Barack Obama and I set out to build lives guided by these values and pass them on to the next generations. Because we want our children, and all children in this nation to know that the only limit to the height of your achievement is the reach of your dreams and your willingness to work for them.*"

Number 45 Jr. and his Russian connection.

Personal note: It is disingenuous to suggest that Donald Trump was ignorant of the Russian meeting held in Trump Towers in New York City.

The subject line on one of the emails points to the purpose of the meeting. CNN, MSNBC, CBS, NBC and other prominent news stations reported that in his response to questions, Number 45 Jr. failed to state all the individuals in attendance. Is it a lie? Or, was it a deliberate omission? No one will state the content of the meeting. However, the meeting was in Trump Towers on the 25ᵗʰ floor (according to MSNBC News) and Number 45's apartment is located on floor 26. It could be argued that he was/is aware of the content of the meeting.

Peter Baker, (July 12, 2017) of New York Times, article Conspiracy or Coincidence? A Timeline Open to Interpretation provides a timeline of Number 45, Jr. Russian meeting, and the event(s) leading up to the meeting.

June 2, 2016: In a speech in San Diego, Mrs. Clinton castigated Mr. Trump for his affinity for Mr. Putin, saying the Republican candidate had an "affection for tyrants" that would make him a poor commander in chief. "If you don't know exactly who you're dealing with, men like Putin will eat your lunch," she said. President Vladimir V. Putin in Moscow last year; as a candidate, Mr. Trump expressed admiration for the Russian president.

June 3: Donald Trump Jr. received an email from Rob Goldstone, a former British tabloid reporter who knew the Trumps and spent a lot of time in Russia in recent years. Citing a Russian contact, Mr. Goldstone offered to help provide "very high level and sensitive information" that would "incriminate Hillary" as "part of Russia and its government's support for Mr. Trump." Mr. Trump replied with interest 17 minutes later. "If it's what you say I love it especially later in the summer," he wrote.

June 7: After several more emails, Mr. Trump and Mr. Goldstone agreed to a meeting at Trump Tower on the afternoon of June 9 with what Mr. Goldstone described as a "Russian government attorney who is flying over from Moscow." Mr. Trump said he would probably be joined by Paul J. Manafort, the campaign chairman, and Jared Kushner, his brother-in-law, who would later become a White House senior adviser.

Rob Goldstone, a publicist, and former British tabloid reporter worked at the 2013 Miss Universe pageant, which Mr. Trump put on in Moscow. (…) That evening, the Republican primary season wrapped up with contests in five states. Mr. Trump, the presidential candidate, took the stage in New York and focused on Mrs. Clinton. "I am going to give a major speech on probably Monday of next week, and we're going to be discussing all of the things that have taken place with the Clintons," he said. "Hillary Clinton turned the State Department into her private hedge fund — the Russians, the Saudis, the Chinese — all gave money to Bill and Hillary and got favorable treatment in return."

June 9: Donald Trump Jr., Mr. Manafort, and Mr. Kushner met with Natalia Veselnitskaya, a Russian lawyer who, contrary to Mr. Goldstone's email, did not openly work for the state but was a former prosecutor with deep connections to the Russian government and a history of arguing for Russian interests. In an initial statement to The New York Times, the younger Mr. Trump said Ms. Veselnitskaya primarily discussed a ban on American families seeking to adopt Russian children imposed by Mr. Putin as retaliation for American sanctions on Russians suspected of human rights abuses. Donald Trump Jr. later acknowledged that he had agreed to the meeting because he believed Ms. Veselnitskaya would provide the campaign with incriminating information about Mrs. Clinton. Only after an inquiry by The Times prompted him to release his emails did it become clear that he had been told that the information was coming from the Russian government. Ms. Veselnitskaya, for her part, has maintained that nothing about the campaign was discussed, and she said she provided no incriminating information about Mrs. Clinton. Natalia Veselnitskaya, a Russian lawyer, met with Donald Trump Jr., Paul J. Manafort, and Jared Kushner at Trump Tower in Manhattan in June 2016. (Credit Yury Martyanov/Agence France-Presse) In an interview on Fox News on Tuesday night, the younger Mr. Trump said that Ms. Veselnitskaya's discussion was "sort of nonsensical, inane and garbled," and that he had concluded the original email "was probably some bait and switch" to get him to take the meeting. He said Mr. Kushner left the meeting within 10 minutes, while Mr. Manafort spent most of the time looking at his phone. Mr. Trump said he did not mention the meeting to his father. "There was nothing to tell," he said. "It was literally just a wasted 20 minutes, which was a shame." At 4:40 p.m. that day, or roughly right after the meeting, if it began at 4 p.m. as scheduled, the elder Mr. Trump posted a message on Twitter jabbing Mrs. Clinton about email messages that had been deleted from her private server on the grounds that they were personal and not about government business.

June 13: Mr. Trump, the candidate, ended up not giving the "major speech" about Mrs. Clinton's dealings with Russia and other countries, despite his promise. Mrs. Clinton's campaign spent the day waiting for the attack. "We were very concerned about it," Ms. Palmieri said. "We put a team together." The campaign figured the attack would be a reprise of some of the allegations raised a year earlier in a book called "Clinton Cash" by Peter Schweizer, so Mrs. Clinton's advisers drafted responses and recruited surrogates to go on television to defend her.

"Then the day came, and I was in the room with Hillary, and we're monitoring what he said, and he didn't do anything," Ms. Palmieri said. On Wednesday, the White House said Mr. Trump had switched speeches because of the mass shooting at an Orlando, Fla., nightclub the day before. Mrs. Clinton in Cleveland in June 2016. Her campaign attacked Mr. Trump after he failed to deliver a promised "major speech" about her dealings with Russia. Credit Eric Thayer for the New York Times

June 15: A hacker calling himself Guccifer 2.0 posted opposition research and donor documents stolen from the Democratic National Committee. A cybersecurity firm that investigated the breach concluded that Russia was behind it. "Too bad the D.N.C. doesn't hack Crooked

Hillary's 33,000 missing emails," Mr. Trump, the candidate, said in a statement.

July 22: The activist group WikiLeaks posted nearly 20,000 emails from senior Democratic National Committee officials. Intelligence officials have said that the emails were taken from the party's computer system by Russian hackers. The same day, Mr. Trump delivered the speech denouncing Mrs. Clinton's ethics that he had promised earlier, relying mainly on "Clinton Cash" and other known controversies linked to her.

July 24: In an interview on CNN, Donald Trump Jr. dismissed Democratic suggestions that the Russians were trying to hurt Mrs. Clinton and help his father. "It's disgusting," he said. "It's so phony." He added: "I can't think of bigger lies. But what exactly goes to show you what the D.N.C. and what the Clinton camp will do. They will lie and do anything to win."

July 27: The elder Mr. Trump publicly dared Russia to hack Mrs. Clinton's emails. "Russia, if you're listening, I hope you're able to find the 30,000 emails that are missing," he said. "I think you will probably be rewarded mightily by our press." Advisers later said he was only joking.

CHAPTER SIX

A Timeline: Russia and President Trump

To keep everything in one location, here's an updated summary (so far) Steven Harper, Bill Moyers of Salon:

- 1979: Roger Stone is introduced to Donald Trump by notorious attorney Roy Cohn. [Added March 27, 2017]
- 1980: Roger Stone founds a lobbying practice with Paul Manafort; Trump becomes one of Stone's first clients. In the 1980s, Trump hires Manafort as his lawyer on gambling and real estate issues. By 1988, Stone is one of Trump's closest advisers. [Added March 27, 2017]
- Trump's efforts to develop business in Russia date to 1987. In 1996, he applies for his trademark in that country. Discussing ambitions for a Trump hotel in 2007, he declares, "We will be in Moscow at some point."
- August 1998: Russia defaults on its debt and its stock market collapses. As the value of the ruble plummets, Russian millionaires scramble to get money out of their country and into New York City, where real estate provides a safe haven for overseas investors. [Added March 20, 2017]
- October 1998: Demolition of a vacant office building near the United Nations headquarters is making way for Trump World Tower. Donald Trump begins selling units in the skyscraper, which is scheduled to open in 2001 and becomes a prominent depository of Russian money. By 2004, one-third of the units sold on the 76th through 83rd floors of Trump World Tower

45

involve people or limited liability companies connected to Russia or neighboring states. Assisting Trump's sales effort is Ukrainian immigrant Semyon "Sam" Kislin, who issues mortgages to buyers of multimillion-dollar Trump World Tower apartments. In the late 1970s, Kislin had co-owned an appliance store with Georgian immigrant Tamir Sapir, and they had sold 200 television sets to Donald Trump on credit. By the early 1990s, Kislin had become a wealthy commodities trader and campaign fundraiser for Mayor Rudy Giuliani, who in 1996 appoints him to the New York City Economic Development Corporation. Meanwhile, Sapir makes a fortune as a New York City real estate developer. [Added March 20, 2017]

- 2000: Roger Stone serves as chairman of Donald Trump's presidential exploratory advisory committee. [Added March 27, 2017]

- 2002: Russian-born Felix H. Sater and his company, Bayrock Group — a Trump Tower tenant — begin working with Trump on a series of real estate development deals, one of which becomes the Trump SoHo. Another development partner in Trump SoHo is the Sapir Organization, founded by Tamir Sapir. [Revised March 20, 2017]

- Also, in 2002: Efforts to sell Russians apartments in Trump World Tower, Trump's West Side condominiums, and Trump's building on Columbus Circle expand with presentations in Moscow involving Sotheby's International Realty and a Russian realty firm. In addition to buying units in Trump World Tower, Russians and Russian-Americans flood into another Trump-backed project in Sunny Isles Beach, Florida. In South Florida alone, members of the Russian elite invest more than $98 million in seven Trump-branded luxury towers. [Added March 20, 2017]

- 2005: In a sworn deposition in 2008, Sater testifies that Trump gave Bayrock Group an exclusive deal to develop a project in Russia. "I'd come back, pop my head into Mr. Trump's office and tell him, you know, 'Moving forward on the Moscow deal.' And he would say 'All right... I showed him photos, I showed him the site, showed him the view from the site. It's pretty spectacular." But that early effort to develop a Trump Tower in Moscow fails. [Added March 3, 2017]

- June 2005: Paul Manafort proposes that he undertake a consulting assignment for one of President Vladimir Putin's billionaire oligarchs. Manafort suggests a strategy for influencing politics, business dealings and news coverage inside the United States, Europe and former Soviet republics to benefit Putin's government. [Added March 27, 2017]

- February 2006: Two of Trump's children, Don Jr. and Ivanka, travel to Moscow. According to Sater, Donald Trump Sr. asked him to show them around: "He asked if I wouldn't mind joining them and looking after them while they were in Moscow." He summarizes the attitude of Trump's children as "nice, big city, great. Let's do a deal here." Ten years later — October 2016 — Trump Organization general counsel Alan Garten tells Forbes that the presence of Sater and Trump's adult children in Moscow at the same time had been a coincidence. [Added March 3, 2017.]

- Sept. 19, 2007: As Trump speaks at the launch party for Trump SoHo, Sater and his Bayrock partner, Kazakhstan native Tevfik Arif, stand next to him. [Added March 3, 2017]

- Oct. 15, 2007: In an interview with Larry King, Trump says: "Look at Putin — what he's doing with Russia — I mean, you know, what's going on over there. I mean this guy has done — whether you like him or don't like him — he's doing a great job."

- November 2007: Paul Manafort's firm receives a $455,000 wire transfer from Ukraine Prime Minister Viktor Yanukovych's Party of Regions. Manafort had been hired to improve the image of Putin-backed Yanukovych, who was portraying himself falsely as an anti-corruption reformer seeking to move Ukraine closer to the West. "The West has not been willing to move beyond the Cold War mentality and to see this man and the outreach that he has extended," Manafort says about Yanukovych at the time. Ukraine's richest man — a billionaire industrialist — had introduced Manafort to Yanukovych. [Added April 17, 2017]

- July 2008: As the Florida real estate market began to crash, Trump sells a Florida residence to a Russian oligarch for $95 million, believed to be the biggest single-family home sale in US history. The Russian oligarch never lived in the house and, since then, it has been demolished. Three years earlier, Trump had bought the home at auction for $41 million. [Added March 3, 2017]

- September 2008: Donald Trump Jr. says: "Russians make up a pretty disproportionate cross-section of a lot of our assets... we see a lot of money pouring in from Russia."

- Oct. 14, 2009: Paul Manafort's firm receives a $750,000 wire transfer from Viktor Yanukovych's Party of Regions. The Russian-leaning Yanukovych was running for president and, in February 2010, he won. [Added April 17, 2017]

- January 2010—January 2011: After leaving Bayrock, Sater becomes "senior adviser to Donald Trump," according to his Trump Organization business card. He also has a Trump Organization email address and office. The phone number listed on the card had belonged previously to a lawyer in Trump's general counsel's office. [Added March 3, 2017]

- April 8, 2013: Three Russians whom the FBI later accused of spying on the United States discuss efforts to recruit American businessman Carter Page. According to The Washington Post, "[T]he government's application for the surveillance order targeting Page included a lengthy declaration that laid out investigators' basis for believing that Page was an agent of the Russian government and knowingly engaged in clandestine intelligence activities on behalf of Moscow, officials said." [Added April 17, 2017]

- June 18, 2013: Trump announces that the 2013 Miss Universe beauty pageant, which he owns, will take place in Moscow. The next day, he tweets: "Do you think Putin will be going to The Miss Universe Pageant in November in Moscow — if so, will he become my new best friend?" While preparing for the pageant, Trump says, "I have plans for the establishment of business in Russia. Now, I am in talks with several Russian companies to establish this skyscraper."

- July 8, 2013: After a BBC reporter questions Trump about Felix Sater's alleged prior connections to organized crime, Trump ends the interview. [Added March 3, 2017]

- Oct. 17, 2013: On the Late Show, David Letterman asks Trump, "Have you had any dealings with the Russians?" Trump answers, "Well I've done a lot of business with the Russians…" Letterman continues, "Vladmir Putin, have you ever met the guy?" Trump says, "He's a tough guy. I met him once."

- Nov. 5, 2013: In a deposition, an attorney asks Trump about Felix Sater. "If he were sitting in the room right now, I really wouldn't know what he looked like," Trump answers. When asked how many times he had ever spoken with Sater, Trump says, "Not many." When asked about his July 2013 BBC interview during which he was questioned about Sater's alleged connections to organized crime, Trump says he didn't remember it. [Added March 3, 2017]

- Nov. 11, 2013: Trump tweets, "TRUMP TOWER-MOSCOW is next."

- November 2013: At the Miss Universe pageant, Trump says: "I do have a relationship [with Putin] and I can tell you that he's very interested in what we're doing here today...I do have a relationship with him . . . He's done a very brilliant job in terms of what he represents and who he's represented." While Trump is in Moscow for the pageant, he and Alex Sapir (whose family's company was one of the co-developers of Trump SoHo with Trump and Felix Sater) meet with the Russian real estate developer who had facilitated Trump's $20 million deal to host the Miss Universe contest in Moscow. They discuss plans for a new Trump project in Russia. "The Russian market is attracted to me," Trump tells Real Estate Weekly upon his return. "I have a great relationship with many Russians, and almost all of the oligarchs were in the room." [Added March 3, 2017]

- Feb. 22, 2014: Popular uprisings lead the Ukraine Parliament to oust President Viktor Yanukovych from office for gross human rights violations and dereliction of duty. With the help of Putin's security forces, Yanukovych flees the country. But he leaves behind a handwritten ledger — the "Black Ledger" — with 22 entries for 2007 to 2012 purporting to show $12.7 million in undisclosed cash payments designated for Paul Manafort or his firm from Viktor Yanukovych's Party of Regions. [Added April 17, 2017]

- March 6, 2014: At the 2014 Conservative Political Action Conference, Trump says: "You know, I was in Moscow a couple of months ago. I own the Miss Universe Pageant and they treated me so great. Putin even sent me a present, a beautiful present." On the same day, President Obama signs an executive order imposing sanctions on Russia for its unlawful annexation of Crimea.

- Sometime in 2014: Golf writer and co-author of Arnold Palmer's memoir James Dodson plays golf with Donald and Eric Trump at Trump National Charlotte in North Carolina. In an interview aired May 5, 2017, on Boston's public radio station, Dodson describes the episode, beginning with a question. He asks Donald Trump before the round: "What are you using to pay for these courses?" And he just sort of tossed off that he had access to $100 million. So, when I got in the cart with Eric, as we were setting off, I said, 'Eric, who's funding? I know no banks — because of the recession, the Great Recession — have touched a golf course. You know, no one's funding any kind of golf construction. It's dead in the water the last four or five years.' And this is what he said. He said, 'Well, we don't rely on American banks. We have all the funding we need out of Russia.' I said, 'Really?' And he said, 'Oh, yeah. We've got some guys that really, really love golf, and they're really invested in our programs. We just go there all the time. Now that was three years ago, so it was pretty interesting.'" On May 7, 2017, Eric Trump calls Dodson's claim, "categorically untrue" and "complete garbage." [Added May 8, 2017]

- June 16, 2015: Trump announces he is running for president.

- Aug. 6, 2015: The Trump campaign says it has fired Roger Stone; Stone claims he'd quit. Either way, Stone remains a prominent Trump surrogate for the rest of the campaign. [Added March 27, 2017]

- Aug. 21, 2015: Alabama Sen. Jeff Sessions makes a surprise appearance at a Donald Trump rally and dons a "Make America Great Cap."

- Late summer 2015: A member of Trump's campaign staff calls Lt. Gen. Mike Flynn to ask if he's willing to meet with Trump. Flynn agrees. Later, Flynn says four other Republican presidential candidates also reached out to him: Carly Fiorina, Scott Walker, Ben Carson and Ted Cruz. [Added May 15, 2017]

- September 2015: An FBI special agent contacts the Democratic National Committee to report that at least one DNC computer system had been hacked by an espionage team linked to the Russian government. The agent is transferred to a tech-support contractor at the help desk, who did a cursory check of DNC server logs and didn't reply to follow-up calls from the FBI agent. [Added March 13, 2017]

- Sept. 21, 2015: On Hugh Hewitt's radio program, Trump says, "The oligarchs are under [Putin's] control, to a large extent. I mean, he can destroy them, and he has destroyed some of them... Two years ago, I was in Moscow . . . I was with the top-level people, both oligarchs and generals, and top-of-the-government people. I can't go further than that, but I will tell you that I met the top people, and the relationship was extraordinary." [Added March 3, 2017]

- Sept. 29, 2015: Trump tells Bill O'Reilly: "I will tell you in terms of leadership he [Putin] is getting an 'A,' and our president is not doing so well."

- Nov. 10, 2015: At a Republican primary debate, Trump says: "I got to know [Putin] very well because we were both on 60 Minutes. We were stablemates, and we did very well that night."

- Nov. 30, 2015: When an Associated Press reporter asks Trump about Felix Sater, he answers, "Felix Sater, boy, I have to even think about it. I'm not that familiar with him." Trump refers questions about Sater to his staff. [Added March 3, 2017]

- Dec. 10, 2015: Lt. Gen. Michael Flynn, who would become Trump's national security adviser, sits at Putin's table for the 10th anniversary gala of Russia's state-owned television propaganda network, RT. Flynn had made a paid appearance on the network. For his December speech, he nets $33,500 of the $45,000 paid to his speakers' bureau. For all of 2015, Flynn receives more than $65,000 from companies linked to Russia. [Revised March 20, 2017]

- Late 2015: The British spy agency GCHQ alerts its American counterparts in Washington to suspicious interactions between members of the Trump campaign and known or suspected Russian agents. The GCHQ provides the information as part of a routine exchange of intelligence information. [Added April 17, 2017]

- Feb. 17, 2016: As questions about Russia swirls around Trump, he changes his story: "I have no relationship with [Putin], other than he called me a genius."

- Feb. 28, 2016: Jeff Sessions formally endorses Donald Trump's candidacy for president. Three days later, Trump names Sessions chairman of his campaign's national security advisory committee. [Added March 3, 2017]

- Feb. 29, 2016: Paul Manafort submits a five-page, single-spaced, proposal to Trump. In it, he outlines his qualifications for helping Trump secure enough convention delegates to win the Republican presidential nomination. Manafort describes how he had assisted rich and powerful business and political leaders, including oligarchs and dictators in Russia and Ukraine: "I have managed presidential campaigns around the world." [Added April 10, 2017]

- March 17, 2016: Jeff Sessions discusses Trump's foreign policy positions, saying, "I think an argument can be made there is no reason for the US and Russia to be at this loggerhead. Somehow, someway we ought to be able to break that logjam. Strategically it's not justified for either country." [Added March 3, 2017]

- March 21, 2016: In a Washington Post interview, Trump identifies Carter Page as one of his foreign policy advisers. Page had helped open the Moscow office of investment banking firm Merrill Lynch and had advised Russian state-owned energy giant Gazprom, in which Page is an investor. He blames 2014 US sanctions relating to Russia's annexation of Crimea for driving down Gazprom's stock price. Earlier in March 2016, Iowa tea party activist Sam Clovis had recommended Page to the Trump campaign. [Supplemented April 24, 2017]

- March 29, 2016: On Roger Stone's recommendation, Paul Manafort joins the Trump campaign as convention manager, tasked with lining up delegates. [Added March 27, 2017]

- April 20, 2016: Paul Manafort becomes Trump's campaign manager. Reports surface about his 2007 to 2012 ties to Ukraine's pro-Putin former president, whom Manafort had helped to elect.

- Late April 2016: The Democratic National Committee's IT department notices suspicious computer activity, contacts the FBI, and hires a private security firm, Crowd Strike, to investigate. [Added March 13, 2017]

- May 2016: Crowd Strike determines that highly sophisticated Russian intelligence-affiliated adversaries — denominated Cozy Bear and Fancy Bear — had been responsible for the DNC hack. Fancy Bear, in particular, had indicators of affiliation with Russia's Main Intelligence Department (also known as the GRU). [Added March 13, 2017]

- May 19, 2016: Paul Manafort becomes Trump's campaign chairman and chief strategist. [Added March 27, 2017]

- Early June 2016: At a closed-door gathering of high-powered foreign policy experts visiting with the prime minister of India, Trump foreign policy adviser Carter Page hails Vladimir Putin as a stronger and more reliable than President Obama and touts the positive effect that a Trump presidency would have on US-Russia relations. [Added March 6, 2017]

- June 15, 2016: A hacker with the online persona "Guccifer 2.0" claims credit for the DNC hack and begins posting internal DNC documents on the Guccifer 2.0 website. *CrowdStrike* reiterates its conclusion that the hack had been a Russian intelligence operation. [Added March 13, 2017]

- Also, on June 15, 2016: After the Ukrainian prime minister visits Capitol Hill, Speaker Paul Ryan, R-Wis., House Majority Leader Kevin McCarthy, R-Calif., and other Republican leaders meet privately. During the session, McCarthy says, "I'll guarantee you that's what it is . . . The Russians hacked the DNC and got the [opposition] research they had on Trump." Moments later he says, "There's two people I think Putin pays: Rohrabacher and Trump," referring to Rep. Dana Rohrabacher, R-Calif., who is known in Congress as a fervent defender of Putin and Russia. Some of the lawmakers laugh, but McCarthy continues, "Swear to God." According to a transcript prepared from a tape of the discussion, Ryan immediately interrupts the conversation, saying, "This is an off the record . . . [laughter] . . . NO LEAKS . . . [laughter] . . . alright? This is how we know we are a real family here... What's said in the family, stays in the family." When the Washington Post obtains the transcript in May 2017, it seeks comment from Ryan and McCarthy. Ryan's spokesperson says, "That never happened. The idea that McCarthy would assert this is false and absurd." As detailed in the Post video accompanying its eventual story, the Post reporter then says that he has a transcript of the discussion. Ryan and McCarthy respond that the transcript is false, maybe even made up, and certainly inaccurate. When the reporter says he has listened to an audio recording of the conversation, Ryan's spokesperson says it was a failed attempt at humor. [Added May 18, 2017]

- July 5, 2016: FBI Director James Comey holds a press conference announcing that the bureau has closed its yearlong investigation into Hillary Clinton's use of a private email server while she was secretary of state. Comey says Clinton had been "extremely careless" in handling "very sensitive, highly classified information," but does not recommend prosecution. Typically, when the FBI recommends closing a case, the Justice Department agrees, and no public statement follows. One possible reason for Comey's unusual announcement in the Clinton case could be the contents of a document that the FBI knew Russians had stolen when they hacked the DNC. In it, a Democratic operative suggested that Attorney General Lynch would not let the Clinton email investigation go too far. Comey may have worried that if Lynch announced an end of the investigation, and Russia later leaked the document, voters would doubt the investigation's independence. [Added April 24, 2017]

- July 6, 2016: Another batch of hacked DNC documents appear on the Guccifer 2.0 website. [Added March 13, 2017]

- July 7, 2016: In a lecture at the New Economic School in Moscow, Carter Page criticizes American foreign policy. He says that many of the mistakes spoiling relations between the US and Russia "originated in my own country." Page says he had sought and received permission from the Trump campaign to make the trip. [Revised March 20, 2017]

- July 14, 2016: Another batch of hacked DNC documents appear on the Guccifer 2.0 website. [Added March 13, 2017]

- July 18, 2016: The Washington Post reports that the Trump campaign worked behind the scenes ahead of the Republican Convention on a plank of the 2016 Party Platform that gutted the GOP's longstanding support for Ukrainians' popular resistance to Russia's 2014 intervention.

- Also, on July 18, 2016: At a Heritage Foundation event during the Republican Convention, Jeff Sessions speaks individually with Russian ambassador Sergey Kislyak. [Added March 3, 2017]

- July 19, 2016: Bloomberg reports that over the past year, Trump's debt load has almost doubled from $350 million to $630 million. [Added May 8, 2017]

- Also, during the July 2016 Republican Convention: Carter Page and J.D. Gordon, national security advisers to the Trump Campaign, meet with ambassador Kislyak. They stress that Trump would like to improve relations with Russia. [Revised March 6, 2017]

- July 22, 2016: On the eve of the Democratic National Convention, WikiLeaks releases its first trove of emails stolen from the DNC.

- July 24, 2016: When ABC News' George Stephanopoulos asks whether there were any connections between the Trump campaign and Putin's regime, Trump campaign chair Paul Manafort answers, "No, there are not. And you know, there's no basis to it." [Added March 6, 2017]

- July 25, 2016: Trump tweets, "The new joke in town is that Russia leaked the disastrous DNC emails, which should never have been written (stupid), because Putin likes me." [Added March 3, 2017]

- July 27, 2016: At a press conference, Trump says: "Russia, if you're listening, I hope you're able to find the 30,000 emails that are missing. I think you will probably be rewarded mightily by our press." At the same press conference, he insists: "I never met Putin. I've never spoken to him." In an interview with CBS News, he reiterates: "But I have nothing to do with Russia, nothing to do, I never met Putin, I have nothing to do with Russia whatsoever."

- By the end of July 2016: The FBI has opened an investigation into possible collusion between members of the Trump campaign and Russian operatives. [Added April 24, 2017]

- July 31, 2016: Manafort denies knowing anything about the change in the Republican platform. That afternoon, Boris Epshteyn, Trump's Russian-born adviser, spouts the Kremlin's party line telling CNN: "Russia did not seize Crimea. We can talk about the conflict that happened between Ukraine and the Crimea… But there was no seizure by Russia. That's an incorrect statement, characterization, of what happened."

- Also, on July 31, 2016: On CNN, Jeff Sessions defends Trump's approach to Russia: "This whole problem with Russia is really disastrous for America, for Russia and for the world," he says. "Donald Trump is right. We need to figure out a way to end this cycle of hostility that's putting this country at risk, costing us billions of dollars in defense, and creating hostilities." [Added March 3, 2017]

- And also, on July 31, 2016: Trump tells ABC News he was not involved in the Republican Party platform change that softened America's position on Russia's annexation of Crimea. [Added March 6, 2017]

- Aug. 5, 2016: Trump surrogate Roger Stone writes an article for Breitbart News. Stone argues that Guccifer 2.0 had nothing to do with Russia. [Added March 13, 2017]

- Also, on Aug. 5, 2016: Carter Page's ongoing public criticism of US sanctions against Russia over its actions in Ukraine and his praise for Putin generate increasing attention and concern. In response, Trump campaign spokesman Hope Hicks describes Page as an "informal policy adviser" who "does not speak for Mr. Trump or the campaign." Later that month, after the FBI believes Page was no longer part of the Trump campaign, it obtains a Federal Intelligence Surveillance Act ("FISA") warrant to monitor his communications. The initial 90-day warrant is renewed more than once. [Added April 17, 2017]

- Aug. 6, 2016: NPR confirms the Trump campaign's involvement in the Republican platform change on Ukraine.

- Aug. 8, 2016: Roger Stone addresses a Broward County, Florida Republican Party group. An audience member asks (near the 46-minute mark of the video) about his predictions for an "October surprise" based on materials in the possession of WikiLeaks' founder Julian Assange. In response, Stone says, "I actually have communicated with Assange." [Updated May 8, 2017]

- Aug. 12, 2016: On a #MAGA podcast (around the 7-minute mark), Stone says, "I believe Julian Assange — who I think is a hero fighting the police state — has all of the emails that Huma [Abedin] and Cheryl Mills, the two Clinton aides, thought they had erased. . . . I think Assange has them. I know he has them. And I believe he will expose the American people to this information, you know, in the next 90 days." [Added April 24, 2017]

- Aug. 12, 2016: A batch of hacked Democratic Congressional Campaign Committee (DCCC) documents appear on the Guccifer 2.0 website. [Added March 13, 2017]

- Also, on Aug. 12, 2016: Stone tells Alex Jones that he was "in communication with Julian Assange." Later, Stone continues,

"I am not at liberty to discuss what I have." [Added on April 24, 2017]

- Aug. 13, 2016: After receiving complaints about the publication of private information, Twitter and wordpress.com (host for the Guccifer 2.0 website) suspends the Guccifer 2.0 accounts. [Added March 13, 2017]

- Aug. 14, 2016: Roger Stone tweets, "[N]ow Guccifer 2.0 — why are those exposing the truth banned?" Without explanation, Twitter reinstates the Guccifer 2.0 account. In a private message to Guccifer 2.0, Roger Stone writes, "Delighted you are reinstated. Fuck the State and their MSM lackeys." [Added March 13, 2017]

- Also, on Aug. 14, 2016: The New York Times reports that Ukraine anti-corruption investigators were seeking to identify and recover assets that it claims former President Viktor Yanukovych had stolen from the Ukrainian people. Investigators had discovered the Black Ledger from Yanukovych's pro-Russia Party of Regions. Later, Manafort questions the authenticity of the Black Ledger, claims it had been falsified and asserts that no public evidence exists that he or others received the payments listed on the ledger. [Added April 17, 2017]

- Aug. 15, 2016: Continuing their private exchange, Guccifer 2.0 responds to Stone: "wow thank you for writing back and thank you for an article about me!!! Do you find anything interesting in the docs I posted?" [Added March 13, 2017]

- Also, on Aug. 15, 2016: Guccifer 2.0 releases hacked DCCC documents on primaries in Florida. [Added March 13, 2017]

- Aug. 16, 2016: Stone publishes an article in The Hill and asks Guccifer 2.0 to retweet it, "PLZ RT: How the election can be rigged against Donald Trump — thehill.com/blogs/pundits-..." Guccifer 2.0 responds: "done" and "I read you'd been hacked" [Added March 13, 2017]

- Also on Aug. 16, 2016: With "TRUMP 2000" posters in the background from what appears to be Stone's home office, he again tells radio host Alex Jones (around the 6 1/2-minute mark of the interview) that he has had "back-channel communications" with WikiLeaks and Julian Assange who have "political dynamite" on the Clintons. [Added April 24, 2017]
- Also, on Aug. 16, 2016: In an interview on The Blaze, Stone says he has "communicated" with Julian Assange through a "mutual acquaintance." He continues, "I think that Assange is going to be very influential in this election. . . ." [Added April 24, 2017]
- Aug. 17, 2016: Guccifer 2.0 sends another private message to Stone: "I'm pleased to say that u r great man and I think I gonna read your books" "please tell me if I can help u anyhow it would be a great pleasure to me." [Added March 13, 2017]
- Also, on Aug. 17, 2016: The Associated Press reports that in 2012 Paul Manafort had secretly routed more than $2 million from Ukraine President Yanukovych's governing pro-Russia governing party to two US lobbying firms working to influence American policy toward Ukraine. [Added April 17, 2017]
- Aug. 18, 2016: In a C-SPAN interview, Stone says (around the 48-minute mark of the broadcast) that he's never met Julian Assange, but he has been in touch with him "through an intermediary — somebody who is a mutual friend." He continues, "I expect you're going to see more from Mr. Assange." [Added April 24, 2017]
- Aug. 19, 2016: As reports of Manafort's financial connections to Ukraine intensified, he resigns from the Trump campaign.
- Also Aug. 19, 2016: On the day he resigns from the Trump campaign, Manafort records documents creating Summerbreeze LLC, a shell company that he controls. Shortly thereafter, Summerbreeze receives a $3.5 million loan from

Spruce Capital, a small New York investment firm. Spruce's co-founder is a developer of Trump hotel projects, including Trump International Hotel and Tower in Waikiki. One of Spruce's financial backers, Alexander Rovt, is a billionaire who made his fortune in the privatization of the fertilizer industry in post-Soviet Ukraine. On Feb. 1, 2016, Rovt had shared a Manor College stage forum about Ukraine with Andrii Artemenko, a pro-Putin member of the Ukraine Parliament. In January 2017, Artemenko would resurface at the Manhattan Loews Regency hotel on Park Avenue with long-time Trump business associate Felix Sater and Trump's personal lawyer Michael D. Cohen. During their meeting, Sater gives Cohen a sealed envelope containing Artemenko's Ukrainian-Russian peace plan and asks him to deliver it to Trump national security adviser Michael Flynn. The plan would have leased Crimea to Russia for 50 or 100 years, essentially ceding to Putin the territory he had annexed illegally. [Added April 17, 2017]

- Aug. 21, 2016: Trump surrogate Roger Stone tweets, "Trust me, it will soon the Podesta's time in the barrel. #Crooked Hillary" [Added March 13, 2017]

- Also, on Aug. 21, 2016: Guccifer 2.0 posts hacked DCCC documents on Pennsylvania's congressional primaries. [Added March 13, 2017]

- Also on Aug. 21, 2016: On a local Maryland radio program, Stone denies (around the 6-minute mark of the broadcast) that Guccifer 2.0 is connected to the Russians: "The DNC leaks that nailed Deborah Wasserman Schultz in the heist against Bernie Sanders was not leaked by the Russians, it was leaked by Crucifer [sic] 2, I should say hacked and leaked first by Crucifer 2, well known hacker who is not in the employment of the Russians, and then WikiLeaks. So that whole claim is a canard." [Added April 24, 2017]

- Aug. 26, 2016: In an interview with Breitbart Radio, Stone says (near the 10-minute mark of the interview), "I'm almost confident Mr. Assange has virtually every one of the emails that the Clinton henchwomen, Huma Abedin and Cheryl Mills, thought that they had deleted, and I suspect that he's going to drop them at strategic times in the run up to the rest of this race." [Added April 24, 2017]

- Aug. 29, 2016: Stone tells a local Florida radio interviewer (around the 7-minute mark of the interview), "We're going to, I think, see from WikiLeaks and other leakers see the nexus between the Clinton Foundation and the State Department." About Assange, he says, "Perhaps he has the smoking gun that makes this handcuff time." [Added April 24, 2017]

- Aug. 31, 2016: Guccifer 2.0 posts documents hacked from House Minority Leader Nancy Pelosi's personal computer. [Added March 13, 2017]

- Sept. 8, 2016: Jeff Sessions meets Russian ambassador Kislyak in his Senate office. [Added March 3, 2017]

- Sept. 9, 2016: Guccifer 2.0 sends Roger Stone a link to a blog post about voter turnout, along with this message: "Hi what do you think of the info on the turnout model for the democrat's entire presidential campaign? Basically, how it works is there are people who will vote party line no matter what and there are folks who will actually make a decision. The basic premise of winning an election is turnout your base (marked turnout) and target the marginal folks with persuadable advertising (marked persuadable). They spend millions calculating who is persuadable or what we call a 'soft democrat' and who is a 'hard democrat.'" [Added March 13, 2017]

- Sept. 15, 2016: Guccifer 2.0 posts hacked DCCC documents on New Hampshire, Ohio, Illinois and North Carolina. [Added March 13, 2017]

- Sept. 16, 2016: Stone says on Boston Herald Radio (around the 12-minute mark), "I expect Julian Assange and the WikiLeaks people to drop a payload of new documents on Hillary on a weekly basis fairly soon. And that of course will answer the question of exactly what was erased on that email server." He says he's in touch with Assange "through an intermediary." He also says that Hillary Clinton's association with Putin and Russia's oligarchs was "far more troubling to me than Donald Trump's." [Added April 24, 2017]

- Sept. 23, 2016: Guccifer 2.0 posts hacked DCCC documents on Chairman Rep. Ben Ray Lujan. [Added March 13, 2017]

- Also, on Sept. 23, 2016: Michael Isikoff of Yahoo News reports US intelligence officials are seeking to determine whether Trump foreign policy adviser Carter Page had opened up private communications with senior Russian officials, including talks about the possibility of lifting economic sanctions if Trump became president. [Added April 17, 2017]

- Sept. 25, 2016: Carter Page writes to FBI Director James Comey that in 2016 he "had not met with any sanctioned official in Russia. . . ." [Added April 17, 2017]

- Sept. 26, 2016: Amid accusations that he has ties to Russia, Carter Page takes a leave of absence from the Trump campaign. [Added April 17, 2017]

- Sept. 28, 2016: FBI Director Comey appears before the House Judiciary Committee and refuses to answer questions about whether the bureau is investigating connections between members of the Trump campaign and Russia. "We do not confirm or deny investigations," Comey says. [Added April 24, 2017]

- Oct. 1, 2016: Six days before WikiLeaks releases emails that Russian hackers had acquired from Clinton campaign manager John Podesta's email account, Trump's informal adviser and surrogate Roger Stone tweets, "Wednesday@HillaryClinton is done. #Wikileaks."

- Oct. 4, 2016: Trump tweets: "CLINTON'S CLOSE TIES TO PUTIN DESERVE SCRUTINY."

- Also, on Oct. 4, 2016: Guccifer 2.0 posts documents hacked from the Clinton Foundation. [Added March 13, 2017]

- Oct. 7, 2016: In a joint statement, the Department of Homeland Security and the Director of National Intelligence says, "The US Intelligence Community (USIC) is confident that the Russian Government directed the recent compromises of emails from US persons and institutions, including from US political organizations . . . We believe, based on the scope and sensitivity of these efforts, that only Russia's senior-most officials could have authorized these activities." But two other stories dominate the news cycle: WikiLeaks begins publishing stolen emails from the account of Hillary Clinton campaign chairman John Podesta, and Trump's infamous Access Hollywood tapes become public.

- Oct. 12, 2016: Roger Stone tells NBC News, "I have back-channel communications with WikiLeaks."

- Oct. 19, 2016: During the third presidential debate, Trump dismisses the Oct. 7 US intelligence findings: "[Clinton] has no idea whether it is Russia, China or anybody else . . . Our country has no idea." And he says this: "I don't know Putin. I have no idea . . . I never met Putin. This is not my best friend."

- Oct. 28, 2016: In a letter to key leaders in the House and Senate, FBI Director Comey says that in connection with the bureau's closed investigation into Hillary Clinton's private email server, it was reviewing emails on a computer belonging to Clinton adviser Huma Abedin. Comey says nothing about the ongoing FBI investigation into connections between the Trump campaign and Russia. [Added April 24, 2017]

- Oct. 30, 2016: According to reporting by MSNBC's Rachel Maddow, the $100 million plane belonging to the Russian oligarch who had bought a Florida residence from Trump for $95 million in 2008 was in Las Vegas on the same day Trump was holding a rally there. [Added March 6, 2017]

- Oct. 31, 2016: Asked about news reports that the FBI was investigating connections between the Trump campaign and Russia, former campaign manager Manafort says, "None of it is true . . . There's no investigation going on by the FBI that I'm aware of." [Added March 6, 2017]

- Nov. 3, 2016: According to reporting by MSNBC's Rachel Maddow, the plane belonging to the Russian oligarch who had bought a Florida residence from Trump for $95 million in 2008 was at the single-runaway airport near Concord, North Carolina, where Trump was holding a rally. [Added March 6, 2017]

- Nov. 5, 2016: In a letter to key leaders in Congress, Comey confirms that the FBI has completed its review of the additional Abedin emails and, as a result, has not changed its earlier recommendation not to recommend prosecuting Clinton for her use of a private email server. [Added April 24, 2017]

- Nov. 8, 2016: Election Day.

- Nov. 9, 2016: After Putin announced Trump's election victory, Russia's Parliament erupts in applause.

- Nov. 10, 2016: Russia's deputy foreign minister admits that during the campaign, the Kremlin had continuing communications with Trump's "immediate entourage."

- Nov. 10, 2016: During their first meeting after the election, President Obama warns Trump about appointing Mike Flynn to a top national security post. In 2014, Obama had removed Flynn as the head of the Defense Intelligence Agency. [Added May 15, 2017]

- Nov. 18, 2016: Rep. Elijah E. Cummings, D-Md., Ranking Member of the House Committee on Oversight and Government Reform, sends Trump transition team chair (and Vice President-elect) Mike Pence a letter expressing concerns about NSA-designate Mike Flynn's conflicts of interest. Specifically, Cummings worries about Flynn's work for an entity affiliated with the government of Turkey, as well as a paid trip to Moscow in December 2015 during which Flynn was "highly critical of the United States." [Added May 8, 2017]

- Late November 2016: In a meeting that includes senior Trump transition national security team members, national security adviser-designate Mike Flynn reveals he has scheduled a conversation with Russian Ambassador Sergey Kislyak. In attendance is Marshall Billingslea, a member of the team who had been a senior Pentagon official for President George W. Bush. He warns Flynn that any such communications carry risks because US intelligence agencies are almost certainly monitoring Kislyak's conversations. After the meeting, Billingsea asks national security officials in the Obama White House for a copy of the classified CIA profile of Kislyak. [Added May 8, 2017]

- Early December 2016: In Moscow, Russians arrest a Russian computer security expert and two high-level intelligence officers who worked on cyber operations. They are charged with treason for providing information to the United States. The arrests amount to a purge of the cyber wing of the FSB, successor to the KGB and the main Russian intelligence agency. [Added March 3, 2017]

- Also, in December 2016: Officials in the Obama administration become concerned that the incoming administration would cover up or destroy previously gathered intelligence relating Russia's interference with the election. To preserve that intelligence for future investigations, they spread it across the government. [Added March 3, 2017]
- Also, in December 2016: Russian ambassador Kislyak meet at Trump Tower with Trump's son-in-law Jared Kushner and Trump's NSA-designate Michael Flynn. [Added March 3, 2017]
- Dec. 8, 2016: Carter Page is in Moscow for several days to meet with "business leaders and thought leaders." [Added March 6, 2017]
- Dec. 9, 2016: In response to a Washington Post report that the CIA had concluded Russia had intervened in the election to help Trump win, he says, "These are the same people that said Saddam Hussein had weapons of mass destruction. The election ended a long time ago in one of the biggest Electoral College victories in history. It's now time to move on and 'Make America Great Again."
- Also, on Dec. 9, 2016: Paul Manafort tells CBS News he is not active in the Trump transition. Asked if he is talking to President-elect Trump, Manafort says, "I don't really want to talk about who I'm speaking to, but I'm aware of what's going on." Interviewers also question him about the appearance of his name among the handwritten entries in the Ukraine Party of Regions' Black Ledger from 2007 to 2012 (purporting to show more than $12 million in payments to him). Manafort responds that the ledger was fabricated. [Added April 17, 2017]
- Dec. 11, 2016: Trump praises Rex Tillerson, chairman of ExxonMobil and recipient of Russia's "Order of Friendship" Medal from Vladimir Putin in 2013, as "much more than a

business executive" and a "world-class player." Trump says Tillerson "knows many of the players" and did "massive deals in Russia" for Exxon. Two days later, Trump nominates him to be secretary of state.

- Also, on Dec. 11, 2016: Asked about the earlier US intelligence report on hacking, Trump says, "They have no idea if it's Russia or China or somebody. It could be somebody sitting in a bed some place. I mean, they have no idea."

- Dec. 12, 2016: While in Moscow, Trump's former campaign surrogate Jack Kingston meets with Russian businessmen to discuss what they might expect from a Trump administration. "Trump can look at sanctions," Kingston says. "They've been in place long enough." [Added March 3, 2017.]

- Dec. 13, 2016: NBC News' Richard Engel reports from Moscow on Trump's secretary of state pick, Rex Tillerson. Former Russian Energy Minister Vladimir Milov tells Engel that Tillerson was a "gift for Putin."

- Dec. 29, 2016: On the same day President Obama announces sanctions against Russian in retaliation for its interference in the 2016 election, national security adviser-designate Lt. Gen. Flynn places five phone calls to the Russian ambassador.

- Dec. 30, 2016: After Putin makes a surprise announcement that Russia would not retaliate for the new sanctions, Trump tweets, "Great move on delay (by V. Putin) — I always knew he was very smart."

- Jan. 3, Jan. 4 and Jan. 5, 2017: Trump tweets a series of attacks on the integrity of the US intelligence community's findings that Russia had hacked the election.

- Also, on Jan. 4, 2017: NSA-designate Mike Flynn tells the transition team's chief counsel Donald F. Mc Gahn II that he is under federal investigation for secretly working as a paid lobbyist for Turkey. Flynn's lawyer followed up but did not get a call back until Jan. 6. [Added May 18, 2017]

- Jan. 6, 2017: The CIA, FBI and NSA release their unclassified report, concluding unanimously, "Vladimir Putin ordered an influence campaign in 2016 aimed at the US presidential election." The three intelligence agencies agree that "the Russian government aspired to help President-elect Trump's election chances when possible." The report also states that WikiLeaks had been Russia's conduit for the effort, writing "We assess with high confidence that Russian military intelligence (General Staff Main Intelligence Directorate or GRU) used the Guccifer 2.0 persona and DCLeaks.com to release US victim data obtained in cyber operations publicly and in exclusives to media outlets and relayed material to WikiLeaks." [Updated March 13, 2017]

- Jan. 10, 2017: At Jeff Sessions' confirmation hearing to become attorney general, Sen. Al Franken, D-Minn., asks him, "If there is any evidence that anyone affiliated with the Trump campaign communicated with the Russian government in the course of this campaign, what will you do?" Sessions answers: "I'm not aware of any of those activities. I have been called a surrogate at a time or two in that campaign and I did not have communications with the Russians, and I'm unable to comment on it." [Updated March 4, 2017]

- Jan. 11, 2017: At his first news conference, Trump says, "As far as hacking, I think it was Russia. But I think we also get hacked by other countries and other people." The final question of Trump's first news conference comes from Ann Compton of ABC News: "Mr. President-elect, can you stand here today, once and for all, and say that no one connected to you or your campaign had any contact with Russia leading up to or during the presidential campaign?" Trump never answered her. Away from cameras and heading toward the elevators, he reportedly says, "No," his team didn't have contact with Russia.

- Jan. 11, 2017: Sheri Dillon, Trump's outside lawyer and a partner in the Morgan, Lewis & Bockius law firm, presents the plan to deal with Trump's business conflicts of interest during his presidency. The plan allows Trump to retain beneficial ownership in all of his businesses. Across the political spectrum, legal experts agree the plan is a sham because, among other things, it does not require Trump to divest his holdings. [Added May 15, 2017]

- Jan. 13, 2017: In response to The Washington Post's article about Flynn's Dec. 29 conversations with the Russian ambassador, press secretary, Sean Spicer says it was only one call. They "exchanged logistical information" for an upcoming call between Trump and Vladimir Putin after the inauguration.

- Jan. 15, 2017: "We should trust Putin," Trump tells The Times of London. Expressing once again his skepticism about NATO, Trump lambastes German Chancellor Angela Merkel.

- Also on Jan. 15, 2017: Appearing on CBS' "Face the Nation", Vice President Pence says Flynn's call to the Russian ambassador on the same day President Obama announced new sanctions was "strictly coincidental," explaining: "They did not discuss anything having to do with the United States' decision to expel diplomats or impose censure on Russia. . . . What I can confirm, having to spoken with [Flynn] about it, is that those conversations that happened to occur around the time that the United States took action to expel diplomats had nothing whatsoever to do with those sanctions."

- Jan. 19, 2017: The New York Times reports that former Trump campaign manager Paul Manafort, along with advisers Roger

Stone and Carter Page, are under investigation in connection with possible links to Russia. [Added March 3, 2017]

- Jan. 20, 2017: Trump is inaugurated.

- Jan. 22, 2017: Lt. Gen. Michael Flynn was sworn in as national security adviser, a position that does not require Senate confirmation.

- Jan. 23, 2017: At Sean Spicer's first press briefing, Spicer says that none of Flynn's conversations with the Russian ambassador touched on the Dec. 29 sanctions. That got the attention of FBI Director James Comey. According to The Wall Street Journal, Comey convinced acting Attorney General Sally Yates to delay informing the White House immediately about the discrepancy between Spicer's characterization of Flynn's calls and US intelligence intercepts showing that the two had, in fact, discussed sanctions. Comey reportedly asked Yates to wait a bit longer so that the FBI could develop more information and speak with Flynn himself. The FBI interviews Flynn shortly thereafter.

- Jan. 24, 2017: According to a subsequent article in The Washington Post, Flynn reportedly denied to FBI agents that he had discussed US sanctions against Russia in his December 2016 calls with the Russian ambassador.

- Jan. 26, 2017: Acting Attorney General Sally Yates informs White House counsel Don McGahn that Flynn had made misleading statements about his late December conversations with the Russian ambassador. Sean Spicer later says Trump and a small group of White House advisers were "immediately informed of the situation."

- Jan. 26, 2017: Acting Attorney General Sally Yates informs White House Counsel Don McGahn that, based on recent public statements of White House officials including Vice President Mike Pence, Flynn had lied to Pence and others about his late-December conversations with Russian Ambassador Kislyak. According to Sean Spicer, Trump and a small group of White House advisers were "immediately informed of the situation." [Added May 15, 2017]

- Jan. 27, 2017: McGahn asks Yates to return to the White House for another discussion about Flynn. He asks Yates, "Why does it matter to the Department of Justice if one White House official lies to another?" Yates explains that Flynn's lies make him vulnerable to Russian blackmail because the Russians know that Flynn lied and could probably prove it. [Added May 15, 2017]

- Also, on Jan. 27, 2017: In a one-on-one White House dinner that Trump had requested, he asks FBI Director Comey for a pledge of personal loyalty. Comey, who was uneasy about even accepting the dinner invitation, responds that he can't do that, but he can pledge honesty. Afterward, Comey describes the dinner to several people on the condition that they not disclose it while he remains director of the FBI. [Added May 15, 2017]

- Late January 2017: At the Manhattan Loews Regency hotel on Park Avenue, Trump's personal attorney, Michael D. Cohen, meets with Felix Sater and Andrii Artemenko, a pro-Putin lawmaker from Ukraine. Artemenko and Sater gave Cohen a peace plan whereby Russia would lease Ukraine for 50 or 100 years and, eventually, get relief from US sanctions. According to The New York Times, Cohen says he would give the plan to national security adviser Michael Flynn. Responding to questions from The Washington Post, Cohen denies that statement, calling it "fake news." [Added March 3, 2017]

- Jan. 30, 2017: Trump fires Acting Attorney General Sally Yates. According to his statement, the reason was that she had "betrayed the Department of Justice" by refusing to defend Trump's travel ban in court.

- Feb. 8, 2017: Flynn tells reporters at The Washington Post he did not discuss US sanctions in his December conversation with the Russian ambassador.
- Also, on Feb. 8, 2017: Jeff Sessions, the first senator to endorse Trump's candidacy and the former chair of the Trump campaign's national security advisory committee, becomes attorney general. Every Republican senator and Democrat Joe Manchin of West Virginia votes to confirm him. During the confirmation process, Sessions had said he was "not aware of a basis to recuse myself" from the Justice Department's Russia-related investigations of Trump.
- Feb. 9, 2017: Through a spokesman, Flynn changes his position: "While [Flynn] had no recollection of discussing sanctions, he couldn't be certain that the topic never came up."
- Feb. 10, 2017: Trump tells reporters he was unaware of reports surrounding Flynn's December conversations with the Russian ambassador.
- Also, on Feb. 10, 2017: On the Friday preceding Trump's weekend at Mar-A-Lago, the plane belonging to the Russian oligarch who had bought a Florida residence from Trump for $95 million in 2008 flies from the south of France to Miami International Airport. [Added March 6, 2017]
- Feb. 13, 2017: The Washington Post breaks another story: Then-acting Attorney General Sally Yates had warned the White House in late January that Flynn had mischaracterized his December conversation with the Russian ambassador, and that it made him vulnerable to Russian blackmail. Later that evening, Flynn resigns.
- Feb. 14, 2017: The New York Times corroborates the Russian deputy foreign minister's admission on Nov. 10. Based on information from four current and former American officials,

The Times reports, "Members of the Trump campaign and other Trump associates had repeated contacts with senior intelligence officials in the year before the election." Meanwhile, advisers to Attorney General Jeff Sessions reiterates his earlier position: Sessions sees no need to recuse himself from the ongoing Justice Department investigations into the Trump/Russia connections.

- Also, on Feb. 14, 2017: Press secretary Sean Spicer denies that anyone in the Trump campaign had any contacts with Russia during the campaign. [Added March 3, 2017]

- Also, on Feb. 14, 2017: In a private Oval Office meeting, Trump asks FBI Director Comey to halt the investigation of former NSA Mike Flynn. According to Comey's contemporaneous memorandum, Trump says, "I hope you can see your way clear to letting this go, to letting Flynn go. He is a good guy. I hope you can let this go." According to the memo, Trump tells Comey that Flynn had done nothing wrong. Comey does not say anything to Trump about halting the investigation, replying only: "I agree he is a good guy." [Added May 17, 2017]

- Feb. 15, 2017: Trump tweets a series of outbursts attacking the Trump/Russia connection as "nonsense," diverting attention to "un-American" leaks in which "information is illegally given out by 'intelligence' like candy." Shortly thereafter, Utah Rep. Jason Chaffetz and other congressional Republicans formally ask the Justice Department's inspector general to investigate the leaks, but they and their GOP colleagues resist the creation of an independent bipartisan commission with the power to convene public hearings and discover the truth about the Trump/Russia connections.

- Also, on Feb. 15, 2017: During an afternoon appearance with Israeli Prime Minister Benjamin Netanyahu, Trump refuses to answer questions about connections between his presidential campaign and Russia. That evening, The New York Times reports that Trump is planning to appoint Stephen Feinberg, a billionaire hedge fund manager and Trump ally, to lead "a broad review of American intelligence agencies." Feinberg has no prior experience in intelligence or government, but he has close ties to Steve Bannon and Jared Kushner.

- And also, on Feb. 15, 2017: Chief of staff Reince Priebus asks FBI Deputy Director Andrew McCabe to rebut publicly The New York Times' story about Trump aides' contacts with Russia during the campaign. McCabe and FBI Director Comey refuse. The White House then asks senior intelligence officials and key lawmakers — including the chairmen of the Senate and House intelligence committees conducting the Trump/Russia investigation — to contact the media and counter the Times story themselves. [Added March 3, 2017]

- And also, on Feb. 15, 2017: Former Trump campaign foreign policy adviser Carter Page deny having any meetings in 2016 with Russian officials inside or outside Russia: "I had no meetings, no meetings." [Added March 6, 2017]

- Feb. 16, 2017: Trump continues his diversionary twitter assault on the intelligence leaks that were fueling intensified scrutiny of his Russia connections. At Trump's afternoon press conference, he says: "I own nothing in Russia. I have no loans in Russia. I don't have any deals in Russia… Russia is fake news. Russia — this is fake news put out by the media." Reporters ask repeatedly about anyone else involved with Trump or his campaign. "No," Trump says. "Nobody that I know of."

- Feb. 17, 2017: FBI Director Comey meets privately with members of the Senate Intelligence Committee to discuss the Russia investigation. Immediately thereafter, the Committee sends a letter asking more than a dozen agencies, organizations and individuals — including the White House — to preserve all communications related to the Senate panel's investigation into Russian interference in the 2016 election. [Added March 3, 2017]

- Also, on Feb. 17, 2017: The Senate Intelligence Committee sends Roger Stone a letter asking him to preserve any records he had in connection with the Committee's inquiry into Russia's interference in the US election. [Added March 20, 2017]

- Feb. 20-26, 2017: Trump continues his attacks on the media and the FBI leaks that were generating the Trump/Russia stories. [Added March 3, 2017]

- Feb. 25, 2017: Nigel Farage, ex-leader of the UK Independence Party, key Brexit campaigner and one of Donald Trump's most visible foreign supporters during and after the presidential campaign, dines with Trump, daughter Ivanka, son-in-law Jared Kushner and Florida Gov. Rick Scott at the Trump International Hotel in Washington. [Added March 13, 2017]

- Feb. 26, 2017: NBC's Chuck Todd notes a pattern: Trump's attacks on the press followed immediately after a new and unflattering Trump/Russia story breaks. [Added March 3, 2017]

- Feb. 28, 2017: On a party line vote, the House Judiciary Committee kills Rep. Jerrold Nadler's Resolution of Inquiry calling for Trump to provide documents relating to Trump/Russia connections and his business conflicts of interest. [Added March 3, 2017]

- Also on Feb. 28, 2017: More than 10 days after the Senate Intelligence Committee had requested that the White House and other agencies preserve Trump/Russia-related communications, the White House counsel's office instructs Trump's aides to preserve such materials, according to a March 1 report by the Associated Press. [Added March 3, 2017]

- March 1, 2017: In response to reports in The Washington Post, The Wall Street Journal and The New York Times about Jeff Sessions' pre-election contacts with the Russian ambassador, Sessions issues a statement saying he "never met with any Russian officials to discuss any issues of the campaign." [Added March 3, 2017]

- March 2, 2017: Trump says he has "total confidence" in Jeff Sessions and he shouldn't recuse himself from the Russia investigation. An hour later, Sessions recuses himself "from any existing or future investigations of any matters related in any way to the campaigns for President of the United States." [Revised March 13, 2017]

- Also, March 2, 2017: Despite an earlier denial, former Trump campaign foreign policy adviser Carter Page admits to meeting with Russian ambassador Kislyak during the campaign. Another adviser, J.D. Gordon, admits that he'd met with Kislyak during the Republican Convention in July. Gordon says he had successfully urged changes in the party platform that Trump had sought to soften US policy regarding Ukraine. [Added March 6, 2017]

- March 4, 2017: Trump is reportedly furious that Jeff Sessions had recused himself from the Trump/Russia investigation. He unleashes a tweetstorm, claiming that President Obama had wiretapped his phones during the presidential campaign. Stunned by Trump's outburst, White House staffers begin searching for evidence to support his false wiretap claim. Among those reportedly involved in the effort are White House Counsel Donald McGahn II and Ezra Cohen-Watnick, a 30-year-old Trump transition team member whom former national security adviser Mike Flynn had brought to the White House as senior director for intelligence programs. [Revised April 3, 2017]

- Also, on March 4, 2017: Stone tweets — then deletes — about his communications with Assange: "[N]ever denied perfectly legal back channel to Assange who indeed had the goods on #Crooked Hillary." Forty minutes later, the tweet was gone. [Added April 24, 2017]

- March 5, 2017: FBI Director Comey asked the Justice Department to rebut publicly Trump's assertion that President Obama had ordered the wiretapping of Trump's phones. Meanwhile, Sean Spicer announces that neither Trump nor the White House would comment further on Trump/Russia matters until Congress completes an investigation into whether President Obama's executive branch abused its powers during 2016 election. [Added March 6, 2017]

- March 7, 2017: WikiLeaks releases a trove of alleged CIA documents relating to the agency's hacking tools for smartphones, computers and internet-connected devices. [Added March 13, 2017]

- Also, on March 7, 2017: Michael Ellis, 32-year-old general counsel to Nunes' intelligence committee, joins White House Counsel McGahn's office as "special assistant to the president, senior associate counsel to the president and deputy National Security Council legal adviser." [Added April 3, 2017]

- March 8, 2017: Nigel Farage meets with WikiLeaks founder Julian Assange at the Embassy of Ecuador in London, where Assange had found sanctuary since 2012. [Added March 13, 2017]

- March 9, 2017: In an online press conference, Assange threatens to release more documents relating to CIA's hacking capabilities and methods. [Added March 13, 2017]

- Also, on March 9, 2017: When reporters ask Sean Spicer about Nigel Farage's meeting with Julian Assange and whether Farage was delivering a message from Trump, Sean Spicer says, "I have no idea." [Added March 13, 2017]

- March 10, 2017: Trump campaign surrogate Roger Stone admits that in August 2016 he had engaged in private direct messaging with Guccifer 2.0, whom US intelligence agencies later identified as the persona for the Russian hacking operation. Describing the messages as "completely innocuous," Stone says, "It was so perfunctory, brief and banal I had forgotten it." [Added March 13, 2017]

- Also, on March 10, 2017: Mike Flynn's replacement as national security adviser, H.R. McMaster, tells Ezra Cohen-Watnick that he is reassigning him. Unhappy with the decision, Cohen-Watnick appeals to Steve Bannon and Jared Kushner. They intervene and take the issue to Trump, who orders that Cohen-Watnick should remain in his position. [Added April 3, 2017]

- March 12, 2017: John McCain tells CNN's Jake Tapper that former Trump adviser and surrogate Roger Stone "obviously" needs to testify before the Senate Intelligence Committee concerning his communications with Guccifer 2.0. McCain says that Stone should also explain fully his involvement matters relating to Ukraine's pro-Putin former president. [Added March 20, 2017]

- March 13, 2017: Senate Intelligence Committee Chairman Richard Burr says Roger Stone's communications with Guccifer 2.0 are part of the Committee's ongoing investigation and that Stone could be called to testify. [Added March 20, 2017]

- March 14, 2017: House Intelligence Committee Chair Devin Nunes and ranking member Adam Schiff invite former acting Attorney General Sally Yates to testify before their committee at an open hearing on March 28, 2017. [Added April 3, 2017]

- March 15, 2017: Roger Stone is riding in the front passenger seat of a car near Pompano Beach, Florida, when another car broadsides his, shifts gears, backs up and speeds away. In January, Stone had claimed that he was poisoned in late 2016 with polonium, a radioactive material manufactured in a nuclear reactor and used to kill former KGB spy Alexander Litvinenko in 2006. Litvinenko had defected to Britain and become an outspoken critic of Putin. As he lay in a hospital bed, he said Putin had been responsible for his impending death. On Jan. 21, 2016, retired British High Court Judge Sir Robert Owen concluded a House of Commons inquiry and issued a 328-page report finding that Litvinenko's accusation was probably correct. [Added March 20, 2017]

- Also, on March 15, 2017: The chairman of the House Intelligence Committee, Devin Nunes, says the committee has no evidence to support Trump's March 4 wiretapping claim. "I don't think there was an actual tap of Trump Tower," Nunes says. "Are you going to take the tweets literally? If you are, clearly the president is wrong." [Added March 20, 2017]

- Also, on March 15, 2017: On the subject of his wiretapping claims, Trump tells Fox News, "I think you're going to find some very interesting items coming to the forefront over the next two weeks." [Added April 3, 2017]

- March 16, 2017: Senate Intelligence Committee leaders issue a joint statement rebutting Trump's unfounded assertion that President Obama had wiretapped Trump Tower: "Based on the information available to us, we see no indications that Trump Tower was the subject of surveillance by any element of the United States government either before or after Election Day 2016." [Added March 20, 2017]

- March 17, 2017: Roger Stone says he had only just received the letter from the Senate Intelligence Committee, dated Feb. 17, asking him to preserve his records relating to Russian election interference. Quoted in The New York Times, Stone says, "I had never heard allegations that Guccifer 2.0 was a Russian asset until now and am not certain it's correct." He says that his 16 interactions with Guccifer 2.0, which included public Twitter posts and private messages, were all part of "exchanges," not "separate contacts." [Added March 20, 2017]

- March 20, 2017: On the morning of FBI Director Comey's testimony before Congress on his agency's investigation into Russian election interference, Trump tweets: "The Democrats made up and pushed the Russian story as an excuse for running a terrible campaign. Big advantage in Electoral College & lost!" Hours later, Comey testifies that the FBI was investigating Russian interference with election, including "the nature of any links between individuals associated with the Trump campaign and the Russian government and whether there was any coordination between the campaign and Russia's efforts." With respect to Trump's wiretapping claims, Comey says, "I have no information that supports those tweets." [Added March 20, 2017]

- March 20, 2017: In a House Intelligence Committee public hearing, Paul Manafort's name comes up more than two dozen times. [Added March 27, 2017]

- March 21, 2017: In his daily press briefing, Sean Spicer says that, with respect to the Trump campaign, Paul Manafort had "played a very limited role for a very limited period of time." [Added March 27, 2017]

- March 22, 2017: Rep. Devin Nunes, R-Calif., chair of the House Intelligence Committee, bypasses his fellow committee members and goes directly to the White House with alleged evidence that Trump associates may have been "incidentally" swept up in foreign surveillance by American spy agencies. Nunes refuses to release the information or name his sources, even to fellow committee members. And he confirms that he still had seen no evidence to support Trump's claim that President Obama had ordered his wires tapped. [Added March 27, 2017]

- Also on March 22, 2017: In a joint letter to White House chief of staff Reince Priebus, the chairman and ranking member of the House Oversight Committee request information and documents relating to payments that former national security adviser Mike Flynn received from entities affiliated with foreign governments, including Russia and Turkey. [Added May 2, 2017]

- March 23, 2017: In a letter to acting Assistant Attorney General Samuel R. Ramer, Sally Yates' lawyer disagrees with the Justice Department's objections to Yates' anticipated congressional testimony. Associate Deputy Attorney General Scott Schools responds that Yates' testimony is "likely covered by the presidential communications privilege and possibly the deliberative process privilege." But Schools adds that Yates needs only the consent of the White House, not the Justice Department, to testify. [Added April 3, 2017]

- March 24, 2017: Paul Manafort, Carter Page and Roger Stone volunteer to be interviewed by the House Intelligence Committee. [Added March 27, 2017]

- Also, on March 24, 2017: Yates' lawyer writes to White House Counsel McGahn about Yates' upcoming testimony before the House Intelligence Committee. He notes that unless McGahn objects before 10 a.m. on March 27, Yates will appear and answer the committee's questions. [Added April 3, 2017]

- Also, on March 24, 2017: Rep. Nunes cancels public hearings scheduled for March 28. Former Director of National Intelligence James Clapper, former CIA Director John Brennan and former acting Attorney General Sally Yates had been slated to testify before his committee. Nunes postpones their appearances indefinitely. [Added March 27, 2017]

- March 26, 2017: In an interview with ABC's George Stephanopoulos, Roger Stone says, "I reiterate again, I have had no contacts or collusions with the Russians. And my exchange with Guccifer 2.0, based on the content and the timing, most certainly does not constitute collusion." [Added March 27, 2017]

- March 27, 2017: Trump tweets that the House Intelligence Committee should be looking into Bill and Hillary Clinton's ties to Russia: "Trump Russia story is a hoax." [Added April 3, 2017]

- March 30, 2017: The Senate Intelligence Committee opens its hearings into the Trump/Russia investigation. Clinton Watts, senior fellow at George Washington University's Center for Cyber and Homeland Security and former FBI agent, testifies that the committee should follow the money funding misinformation websites. Watts then adds a more ominous suggestion: "Follow the trail of dead Russians," he says. "There's been more dead Russians in the past three months that are tied to this investigation who have assets in banks all over the world. They are dropping dead, even in Western countries." Eight Russian politicians, activists, ambassadors and a former intelligence official have died since Trump's election. Some were apparent assassinations. [Added April 3, 2017]

- Also, March 30, 2017: The New York Times reports that Nunes' sources for the information that he'd reviewed nine days earlier on White House grounds — and then reported to Trump directly without informing anyone on his committee

— are two members of the Trump administration: Ezra Cohen-Watnick (the NSC staffer whose job Trump had saved personally around March 13) and Michael Ellis (who had served as general counsel of Nunes' committee before becoming Trump's "special assistant, senior associate counsel and deputy National Security Council legal adviser" on March 7). [Added April 3, 2017]

- Also, on March 30, 2017: The Wall Street Journal reports that Mike Flynn is seeking immunity from prosecution in return for testifying before congressional intelligence committees. The next day, his lawyer confirms, "Gen. Flynn certainly has a story to tell, and he very much wants to tell it, should circumstances permit." [Added April 3, 2017]

- March 31, 2017: Trump tweets, "Mike Flynn should ask for immunity in that this is a witch hunt (excuse for big election loss), by media & Dems, of historic proportion!" [Added April 3, 2017]

- Also, on March 31, 2017: During an appearance with Bill Maher, Roger Stone denies that Guccifer 2.0 was an arm of Russia. "I've had no contacts with Russians," he insists. [Added April 3, 2017]

- April 5, 2017: In an interview with The New York Times, Trump says, "The Russia story is a total hoax." [Added April 10, 2017]

- April 6, 2017: House Intelligence Committee Chairman Devin Nunes, R-Calif., recuses himself from the Trump/Russia investigation. Texas Rep. Mike Conaway assumes control. [Added April 10, 2017]

- April 12, 2017: The Associated Press confirms that newly obtained financial records show Paul Manafort's firm had received two wire transfers — one in 2007 and another in 2009 — corresponding to two of the 22 entries next to Manafort's name in Ukraine's Party of Regions Black Ledger. Manafort's spokesman says Manafort intended to register retroactively with the US Justice Department as a foreign agent for the work he had done on behalf of political interests in Ukraine through 2014. [Added April 17, 2017]

- April 13, 2017: Former Trump campaign adviser Carter Page tells ABC's George Stephanopoulos he won't reveal who brought him into the Trump campaign. Page also says he didn't recall discussing the subject of easing Russian sanctions in conversations with Russian officials during his July 2016 trip to Moscow. "We'll see what comes out in this FISA transcript," Page says, referring to surveillance collected after the FBI obtained a secret court order to monitor him under the Foreign Intelligence Surveillance Act. "Something may have come up in a conversation... I have no recollection." Later he continues, "Someone may have brought it up. I have no recollection. And if it was, it was not something I was offering or that someone was asking for." Page says that from the time of his departure as an adviser to the Trump campaign through Inauguration Day, he maintained "light contact" with some campaign members. [Added April 17, 2017]

- April 19, 2017: The White House refuses the March 22 bipartisan request from the House Oversight Committee for more information and documents relating to payments that former national security adviser Mike Flynn received from entities affiliated with the Russian and Turkish governments. [Added May 2, 2017]

- April 25, 2017: The Senate Subcommittee on Crime and Terrorism reveals that it has scheduled former acting Attorney General Sally Yates and former Director of National Intelligence James Clapper to testify on May 8, 2017. [Added May 2, 2017]

- April 25, 2017: The Senate confirms Rod Rosenstein as deputy attorney general. Because Attorney General Jeff Sessions had recused himself from matters relating to the 2016 presidential election, including the Trump/Russia investigation, Rosenstein becomes the top Justice Department official supervising FBI Director Comey on that investigation. [Added May 15, 2017]

- April 28, 2017: The chair and vice chair of the Senate Intelligence Committee send letters to several former Trump campaign advisers, including Carter Page, Mike Flynn, Paul Manafort and Roger Stone. Among other requests, the letters ask for a "list of all meetings between you and any Russian official or representative of Russian business interests which took place between June 16, 2015 and Jan. 20, 2017." The letters also request information about any such meetings of which they are aware, as well as all documents relating to Trump campaign communications with Russian officials or business representatives. The committee also seeks information about any financial and real estate transactions related to Russia from June 15, 2015 through Trump's inauguration. [Added May 8, 2017]

- April 29, 2017: In an interview airing on Trump's 100th day in office, he tells CBS' John Dickerson, "The concept of Russia with respect to us [the Trump campaign] is a total phony story." Dickerson then asks, "You don't think it's phony that they, the Russians, tried to meddle in the election?" Trump answers, "That I don't know." Later, Trump says, "I'd love to find out what happened." [Added May 2, 2017]

- May 2, 2017: On the eve of FBI Director James Comey's testimony before the Senate Judiciary Committee, Trump tweets: "FBI Director Comey was the best thing that ever happened to Hillary Clinton in that he gave her a free pass for many bad deeds! The phony . . . Trump/Russia story was an excuse used by the Democrats as justification for losing the election. Perhaps Trump just ran a great campaign?" [Added May 8, 2017]

- May 3, 2017: In response to Sen. Patrick Leahy, D-Vt., who asks FBI Director Comey about Trump's April 29, 2017 interview in which he said that the hacking of the DNC "could've been China, could've been a lot of different groups," Comey answers, "The intelligence community with high confidence concluded it was Russia." [Added May 8, 2017]

- May 5, 2017: The chair and vice chair of the Senate Intelligence Committee issue a joint statement, saying: "Three days ago, Carter Page told Fox News he was cooperating with the Committee's investigation into Russian activities surrounding the 2016 Election. Today we have learned that may not be the case." The statement expresses the hope that Page "will live up to his publicly-expressed cooperation with our effort." [Added May 8, 2017]

- May 6-7, 2017: Trump spends the weekend at his golf course in Bedminster, New Jersey. Since March, he's been fuming over Comey's congressional appearance, in which the FBI director had acknowledged the FBI's ongoing investigation into Trump campaign ties to Russia and had refuted Trump's false claim that President Obama had wiretapped him. In the weeks that followed, Trump grew angrier and talked about firing Comey. At Bed minister, Trump grouses over Comey's May 3 congressional testimony — especially his comment about being "mildly nauseous" at the thought that his actions relating to the Clinton investigation might have affected the outcome of the election. [Added May 15, 2017]

- May 8, 2017: Upon returning to the White House on Monday, Trump tells a few close aides, including Vice President Pence and White House counsel Don McGahn that Comey has to go. According to ABC News, Pence, McGahn, chief of staff Reince Priebus and senior adviser Jared Kushner are members of a small group that begins to prepare talking points about Comey's firing. Trump summons Attorney General Sessions and Deputy Attorney General Rosenstein to the White House, where he instructs them provide a written justification for removing Comey. [Added May 15, 2017]

- Also, on May 8, 2017: With former Acting Attorney General Sally Yates scheduled to testify later in the day. (...)

CHAPTER SEVEN

The Affordable Care Act

September 9, 2009: Transcript: Obama's health care speech-excerpt. Printed by CBS News-Associated Press.

"(...) First, if you are among the hundreds of millions of Americans who already have health insurance through your job, Medicare, Medicaid, or the VA, nothing in this plan will require you or your employer to change the coverage or the doctor you have (...).

(...), it will be against the law for insurance companies to deny you coverage because of preexisting conditions. (...), it will be against the law for insurance companies to drop your coverage when you get sick or water down when you need it the most. They will no longer be able to place some arbitrary cap on the amount of coverage you can receive in a given year or a lifetime. We will place a limit on how much you can be charged for out-of-pocket expenses because, in the United States of America, no one should go broke because they get sick. And insurance companies will be required to cover, with no extra charge, routine checkups, and preventive care, like mammograms and colonoscopies because there's no reason we shouldn't be catching diseases like breast cancer and colon cancer before they get worse. That makes sense, it saves money and it saves lives.

(...), the second part of this plan will finally offer you quality, affordable choices. If you lose your job or you change your job, you'll be able to get coverage. (...) start a small business, you'll be able to get coverage. We'll do this by creating a new insurance exchange- a marketplace where individuals and small businesses will be able to shop for health insurance at competitive prices. Insurance companies will have an incentive to participate in this exchange because it lets them compete for millions of new customers. As one big group, these customers will have greater leverage to bargain. Tax credits will be provided in the exchange for individuals and small businesses who still can't afford the lower-priced insurance. (…). Insurance companies that want access to this new marketplace will have to abide by consumer protections. The exchange will take effect in four years, which will give us time to do it right. In the meantime, for those Americans who can't get insurance today because they have preexisting medical conditions, will immediately offer low-cost coverage that will protect you against financial ruin if you become seriously ill. (…). (…), there still may be those, the young, and the healthy who still want to take the risk and go without coverage. (…)"

Another set of fabrications: Affordable Care Act- Reality check.

Republicans sold it as Obama Care, the Affordable Care Act-ACA (2010) as the worst initiative since the atomic bomb. Ben Carson compared it to slavery. Negativity and fabrications were the hallmark of Number 45, his posse, Mitch McConnell, Washington, DC supporters, and the Republican cliques presented and continued to promote the health care bill in a downward spiral.

Aetna Chairman and C.E.O., Mark Bertolini started the phrase 'death spiral' that became a cry for Republicans to dismantle the Affordable Care Act. He made his case on YouTube. His remarks were a result of the block between Aetna and the Humana merger. Kevin McCoy of USA Today (1/24/17) stated:

"A federal judge Monday temporarily blocked the proposed $37 billion mega-merger between health insurance industry giants Aetna and Humana, ruling that the transaction would reduce competition for consumers. The ruling marks a significant setback for the companies, which in July announced the proposed deal to create the largest seller of Medicare Advantage plans, covering more than 4.1 million seniors.

Humana could get a $1 billion breakup fee from Aetna if the deal falls through. "In this case, the government alleged that the merger of Aetna and Humana would be likely to substantially lessen competition in markets for individual Medicare Advantage plans and health insurance sold on the public exchanges." "US District Court Judge John Bates wrote in his 156-page ruling." After a 13-day trial, and based on careful consideration of the law, evidence, and arguments, the court mostly agrees."

The judge based his decision enjoining the merger on the evidence of "overwhelming market concentration figures" the merger would generate, plus findings of head-to-head competition between Aetna and Humana would be eliminated if the deal were finalized. The decision represents legal vindication for the Justice Department, which was joined by eight states and the District of Columbia in opposing Hartford, Conn.-based Aetna's proposed takeover of Louisville, Ky.-based Humana during the Obama administration. Eight states and the District of Columbia joined the federal action.

A significant reality, according to the 2017 Consumer Report:

"Since its adoption, far fewer Americans have taken the extreme step of filing for personal bankruptcy. Filings have dropped about 50 percent, from 1,536,799 in 2010 to 770,846 in 2016. Those years also represent the time frame when the ACA took effect. Although courts never ask people to declare why they're filing, many bankruptcy and legal experts agree that medical bills had been a leading cause of personal bankruptcy before public healthcare coverage expanded under the ACA. Unlike other causes of debt, medical bills are often unexpected, involuntary, and large.

President-elect Donald Trump (Number 45) said that President Barack Obama's health care law "will fall under its own weight." House Speaker Paul Ryan said the law is "in what the actuaries call a death spiral." And Senate Majority Leader Mitch McConnell said that "by nearly any measure, Obama Care has failed." The problem with all these claims; they are exaggerated, if not downright false. In the process, they are exaggerating the law's very real problems, according to health care experts who largely believe that the Affordable Care Act troubles with high prices and lack of competition could be addressed with bipartisan solutions.

Republicans, who've gained a political advantage from campaigning against the law since its passage in 2010, aren't interested in going along. Instead, they've denounced the law and made the case to repeal it, although there were signs some are getting cold feet now that the reality is upon them. Democrats, too, are guilty of rhetorical excesses around the health care law, often claiming that it's working as intended while downplaying its flaws. But with Republicans in the majority and driving the agenda, here's a look at some of the GOP claims about the law, and how they compare with the facts:

Trump, Ryan, and McConnell: The law will "fall of its own weight," is in a "death spiral" and "has failed." The Facts: Experts agree that the law is not currently in a "death spiral," an actuarial term that refers to a vicious cycle when rising insurance costs force healthy customers out of the marketplace, resulting in still higher prices, which cause even more customers to bail, etc., until the system collapses.

But some say that if the current situation continues, that is a likely or possible scenario. Health care premiums are jumping by double digits this year, and the health care marketplaces created by the law are short on the healthy consumers who make insurance companies profitable.

"It's not a failure in that 20 million people or more have insurance that didn't use to have. Everything else, it's too early to judge," said economist Gail Wilensky, who ran Medicare under former President George H.W. Bush. "To say that the exchange markets remain unstable and in turmoil is an appropriate statement," she said. "To say that they're in a death spiral really depends on what happens." I would argue that a bi-patrician effort needs to be implemented to curtail prescription and medical costs.

The American Academy of Actuaries itself disputed the "death spiral" claim Monday. The group provided a statement from its senior health fellow asserting that high premium increases in many states this year "do not necessarily indicate that a premium spiral is occurring" and could be a one-time adjustment. Ryan: "You cannot fix a fundamentally broken law; you've got to replace it."

The Facts: Experts agree that Congress could fix the law's problems, should it choose to do so. Indeed, many argue that some of the laws' problems can be traced to the decision by Obama and Democrats to push it through on a partisan basis, alienating Republicans who had refused ever since to participate in any attempt to tweak the law to improve it, as would be necessary with any program of such size and complexity. Interestingly, Republicans had dismissed the eighteen months and one hundred and seventy meetings that included every segment of the medical community before the Affordable Care Act was signed.

On Friday, July 28, 2017, during the early morning hours, Number 45, Mitch McConnell and the majority of Republicans did not obtain victory to dispose of the Affordable Care Act. Senator Jon Mc Cain of Arizona, Susan Collins of Maine, and Lisa Murkowski of Alaska cast their vote for people and not a party. Both women received a quasi-reprimand and were ignored by Number 45. National news recorded the thunderous cheers heard outside of Congress when the vote was tallied.

MSNBC News-Morning Joe show identified the failure of passing the Affordable Care Act as Failure Friday. Number 45 has stated repeatedly that Obama Care will implode on its own. I would argue that if this occurs it will be due to contamination from the opposition. Sabotage Saturday would be the game plan should Republicans push towards allocating money through the use of block grants to states for distribution. Moving dollars from the federal government to the states, I would argue it is not a workable solution. I can reflect upon the era of Ronald Reagan concerning a government-funded employment and training program.

For a historical example, the Comprehensive Employment and Training Program (CETA) had been operational since the mid-1960s. Under Ronald Reagan, the program changed to the Private Industry Council (PIC). This transformation allowed states to allocate dollars, and as the manufacturing industry, like, Donna Hanna Coke, Republic Steel, and Bethlehem Steel closed down, workers could register for training, new jobs, even relocation. The majority of workers from the assembly line, foundry, and general labors not holding a journeymen's card, found a challenge to obtaining training, new employment, and many could not afford to relocate. The Dislocated Workers Program lent to support unskilled workers considered dislocated simultaneously. During that time, while working for the Buffalo Urban League, Inc., I was personally told by a senior administrator that the Private Industry Council (PIC) was (is) a Cadillac program if you can get in!

The situation above may be the situation for the underserved, poor, minorities, women, and children. Those who would need medical services would be the least to benefit. Like PIC, agencies that execute health insurance companies in geographic areas will make a tremendous difference.

CHAPTER EIGHT

Presidential comparison: President Barack Obama and Number 45

It is common knowledge that insecurity breeds envy and jealousy. These two behaviors breed hate. Where there is hate, there is disrespect. With disrespect, there are no boundaries. Thus, an examination of Number 45 and his like-minded supporters is in order. In Fact Check. Org. from 2008 through September 19, 2016:

Number 45: Tweets: An 'extremely credible source' has called my office and told me that Barack Obama's birth certificate is a fraud.

3:23 PM - 6 Aug 2012: In the debate, Mitt Romney should ask Obama why his autobiography states "born in Kenya, raised in Indonesia."

2:21 PM - 1 Oct 2012: The wire (2016) "Trump tweeted in 2012 that an "extremely credible source" told him the president's birth certificate "is a fraud," and suggested in 2014 that Obama's college records would show his real "place of birth." He even cast conspiratorial doubts on the sudden death of the Hawaii health director in 2013, two years after she approved the release of Obama's long-form birth certificate." How amazing, the State Health Director who verified copies of Obama's "birth certificate" died in plane crash today. All others lived in a plane crash today. All others lived."

3:32 PM - 12 Dec 2013: How amazing, the State Health Director who verified copies of Obama's "birth certificate" died

3:32 PM - 12 Dec 2013: Again, Fact Check.Org presented some of the biggest lies and disparagements of a president who happened to be an African American:

And Obama has talked about his faith annually at the White House Easter Prayer Breakfast.

None of that has swayed those who continue to wrongly believe that Obama is not a Christian, but also that he is a Muslim. His middle name is "Hussein" after all.

A YouTube video titled "Obama Admits He Is a Muslim" has been viewed nearly 17 million times since April 2009. But it's totally bogus and the result of deceptive editing.

For example, when Obama said, "I am one of them," he doesn't mean that he is a Muslim. He was talking about being like others who either have Muslim relatives or have lived in countries with large Muslim populations. At other times, the video edits out the words "I'm a Christian" and "my Christian faith" from Obama's quotes.

Truth on the Cutting Room Floor, Dec. 4, 2009: Obama also didn't attend a radical "Wahabi" school in Indonesia, as a false viral email claimed. That rumor originated with an inaccurate 2007 Insight Magazine article that said Obama "was educated in a Madrassa as a young boy and has not been forthcoming about his Muslim heritage." CNN interviewed the school's deputy headmaster, Hardi Priyono, who said: "This is a public school. We don't focus on religion."

That same viral email also claimed that Obama was sworn in as a U.S. senator using a Koran. Wrong. Obama reportedly used his own Bible during his swearing-in ceremony in 2005. It was Democratic Rep. Keith Ellison, the first Muslim member of Congress, who used a Koran for his own ceremony in 2007.

Sliming Obama, Jan. 10, 2008: Year after year, concerned readers asked us if Obama had canceled the National Day of Prayer. Our answer was always no. The false rumor started in 2009 when Obama didn't hold a public service in the White House as George W. Bush had done as president. However, Obama issued a National Day of Prayer proclamation in 2009 and every year after. The National Day of Prayer Task Force has also debunked the cancellation claim.

Prayer Day Still Not Cancelled, May 5, 2016

The Viral Spiral of 2010, Dec. 21, 2010

Not only did viral rumors claim that Obama canceled the National Day of Prayer, they also incorrectly faulted Obama for allowing a Muslim prayer event to take place on the grounds of the U.S. Capitol. The permit for the event in September 2009 was issued by the U.S. Capitol Police, not the White House. Obama's only connection to the event was that its chief organizer, Hassen Abdellah, said that he was inspired by the president's inaugural address in January 2009 and a speech Obama gave in June that year.

Muslim Prayer Day Sept. 25, Sept. 21, 2009: And Obama didn't issue a policy in 2009 preventing an Army veteran from speaking at a faith-based event, as an email claimed. The event in question was a fundraiser and had nothing to do with religion. A previously existing policy prohibited the veteran from participating in the fundraiser in an official capacity.

New Army Policy against 'Faith-Based' Events? June 10, 2009: Another viral email expressed outrage at the Obama administration for using "tax dollars to rebuild Muslim mosques around the world." But the State Department's program to preserve overseas cultural landmarks started funding projects under President Bush in 2001. And the program funds the rebuilding of historic churches and temples, too.

Funding Mosques Overseas, March 10, 2011: Obama also didn't write that "I will stand with the Muslims should the political winds shift in an ugly direction" in his 2006 book, "The Audacity of Hope." We looked through the book and found that Obama actually said that he would stand with American immigrants from Pakistan or Arab countries should they be faced with something like the forced detention of Japanese American families in World War II.

Obama's 'Dreams of My Father,' June 3, 2008: And Obama didn't exempt Muslims from having to purchase health insurance as required by the Affordable Care Act, or Obamacare. Nor does Obama's health care law mention the word "dhimmitude," which is an academic concept, not a tenet of the Muslim faith.

'Dhimmitude' and the Muslim Exemption, May 10, 2010: Another viral email misquoted Obama as saying that the U.S. is "no longer a Christian nation." What he actually said was that "whatever we once were, we are no longer a Christian nation — at least, not just." Obama stumbled when he delivered the quote live, but his prepared remarks show that he had intended to say that "we are no longer just a Christian nation," but a nation of many faiths.

Obama and the 'Christian Nation' Quote, Aug. 26, 2008: Yet another viral email wrongly accused Obama of creating a postage stamp commemorating the Muslim holidays Eid al-Fitr and Eid al-Adha. But Obama had nothing to do with the stamp, which was originally announced in 2001 when Bush was president. The stamp has been reissued in different designs several times whenever the postage rate has increased.

Muslim Stamp, Sept. 24, 2009: And while we're on holidays, Obama's White House never stopped referring to the "White House Christmas Tree" as just that. The zombie claims about the White House "holiday tree" was first proved wrong in 2009 but has circulated online annually during the holiday season.

'Holiday Tree' Hooey, Oct. 14, 2009: President-elect Trump acknowledged last year that Obama was born in the U.S. and not in

Kenya. But many Americans still haven't accepted that fact about Obama. It hasn't helped that some have gone out of their way to spread false information about the soon-to-be former president's background.

A widely shared graphic promoted the falsehood that many of Obama's early records are "sealed," including his "original birth certificate." That's nonsense. Obama released a copy of his short-form certification of live birth in 2008 — which FactCheck.org staffers examined and photographed — and then released a copy of his long-form certificate of live birth in 2011. Both versions were validated by state health officials in Hawaii who have said repeatedly that Obama was born there.

Obama's college records aren't sealed, either, as the graphic claimed. It's simply illegal under federal law for Occidental College, Columbia University or Harvard Law School to release Obama's records to the press or the public without Obama's written permission. Presidential candidates almost never voluntarily release such information.

Obama's 'Sealed' Records, July 31, 2012: That viral email on Obama's "sealed" records was mostly a rehash of one we had debunked long before. The earlier version, from a so-called "Colombo," also repeated the fanciful "birther" claim that Obama traveled to Pakistan in 1981 with a non-U.S. passport. According to the theory, U.S. citizens were barred from traveling there at the time, so Obama must have done so with a foreign passport, proving that he wasn't a citizen. Hogwash. Americans traveled to Pakistan with no problem, as shown by a travel piece that appeared in the New York Times in June 1981.

Clueless 'Colombo,' Jan. 18, 2010

More 'Birther' Nonsense: Obama's 1981 Pakistan Trip, June 5, 2009: In addition, an April Fools' Day hoax tricked some into believing that the Associated Press reported that Obama attended Occidental on a

Fulbright scholarship for foreign students, proving that he isn't a U.S. citizen. Not so. The AP confirmed to FactCheck.org that the story attributed to the news agency was a fake.

We received an email asking about Obama's Fulbright scholarship as recently as May 2016, seven years after we first debunked the claim. So, the April Fools' joke is still fooling some people.

Was Obama Born in the USA? May 7, 2009

April Fools'… Still, April 1, 2010: And another viral email questioning what we know about Obama suggested that he didn't attend Columbia University, calling it "very, very strange" that "no one ever came forward" to say that they knew Obama in school. Not only does the university proudly claim Obama as one of its own, but the New York Times wrote about Phil Boerner, who knew Obama in 1979 when they both attended Occidental and then roomed with Obama after they both transferred to Columbia in 1981. Boerner wrote an article for the university's student magazine in 2009, describing how he and Obama met and what it was like living with Obama in New York.

Obama at Columbia University, Feb. 16, 2010

Not Anti-America: We also have seen false claims purporting to show Obama doesn't respect or like the country much. Obama didn't say, as an email claimed, that he wouldn't wear a U.S. flag pin because "I don't want to be perceived as taking sides." Nor did he suggest changing the lyrics of the national anthem because the current version "conveys a war-like message." Those fake quotes were written as a joke by satirist John Semmens for his "semi-news" column.

Obama and the National Anthem, April 22, 2008: And Obama didn't tell his supporters that "we live in the greatest nation in the history of the world" and then ask them to "join with me as we try to change it." That quote, too, was intended as a joke, according to former

National Review contributor Mark Steyn, who said it was sent to him by a reader as "an all-purpose stump speech for the 2008 campaign."

Obama Quote Rumors, Aug. 6, 2008: Obama also didn't ban the Pledge of Allegiance in U.S. public schools. That was a claim from yet another satirical article on a fake news website. But long before we wrote about that, there was the equally fictitious claim that Obama wouldn't even recite the pledge. The support for that one? A 2007 photo of Obama without his hand over his heart during the national anthem, not the Pledge of Allegiance.

Did Not Ban the Pledge, Sept. 2, 2016

Sliming Obama, Jan. 10, 2008: And if Obama wasn't actively being anti-America, he was reading about it, according to another off-base email. The anonymous author of that viral message jumped to the wrong conclusion after seeing a photo of Obama carrying a popular book by journalist Fareed Zakaria. The book, "The Post-American World," is about America's role in a new global era. It isn't an apocalyptic vision of a world "after America," as the email claimed.

Obama's Reading Material, Oct. 1, 2009: This is just a sampling, really, of the bogus claims that have been made up about Obama over eight years. He also didn't create the "Obama phone," call for a "new world order," criminalize free speech, create a "private army," or attempt to declare martial law.

In all, we've written close to 200 Ask Fact Check articles about Obama and the first family, including Bo, the dog. But the attacks on Obama's religion and patriotism stand out — not for what they purported to say about Obama, but for what they say about the biases of people who write and spread such nonsense.

CHAPTER NINE

America's Reality

Since January 20, 2017, America's standard of living entered the 'swamp'. Candidate Number 45 said he was coming to Washington, DC to "drain the swamp". Instead, Number 45 brought the swamp with him. During his campaign, he asked Russia to find 30,000 emails of his opponent, Hillary Clinton. It appeared that during his business dealings with Russia, he opened the door for Vladimir Putin to infiltrate the American political system. He allowed Russian heads of state into the Oval Office and only allowed Russian media to report the meeting. During that meeting, he shared confidential information about Israel. His namesake, 45 Junior, met with a Russian attorney and others to gain information on how to disparage his opponent, Hillary Clinton. MSNBC News, Richard Engle (July 21, 2017) provided an excellent exposé on Russia's strategies and techniques to undermine the American democratic system.

Using the increased cost of health care premiums, the Affordable Care Act was consistently being disparaged by Number 45. It is not out of the realm of possibility to negotiate premium drug costs with insurance companies. There are multi-billion-dollar industries with a cadre of a lobbyist who appear to dictate prescription cost. I wonder how many in Congress receive contributions from these companies. Secondly, because Mc Connell and his supportive Republicans had so much hatred for President Obama, it would not have been beyond the possibility of sabotaging the Affordable Care Act. If anyone is confused about saboteurs, reflect on the initial negative propaganda that was perpetrated by Republicans when the Affordable Care Act was implemented. Many, many white Americans hit the streets with picket signs with comments, "We don't want Obama Care!" The propaganda took an extremely positive nation-wide turn when many Americans and white Americans learned that Obama Care was the Affordable Care Act. I have personally saw more white Americans than any other ethnic group speaking loudly, getting arrested, reading reports about flooding phone lines, and demanding town meetings to keep their health care. Rachel Maddox, of MSNBC, frequently kept America posted on the outcry of health needing families. Interestingly, the world was watching and probably saying, "Wow!" this is America? Other countries provide free health care. Republicans have the Senate, House and, the White House. However, when you have an incompetent and unworthy leader and questionable-smooth talking vice president, what could we expect?! A closer look at Mr. Pence found the following:

On July 18, 2017, Mike Pence gave a speech that was full of falsehoods. During the Retail Advocates Summit in Washington, D.C. He stated, "Congress needs to do their job now!" The meaning was to cause millions of Americans to lose health insurance. Interestingly, CBO scores projected that millions of people would have lost their health care if Republicans repealed and replaced the Affordable Care Act. How cold-hearted, mean-spirited, and downright un-American. Trump, Pence, Republican Majority Leader, Mc Connell, and others talk about what Americans expect. To place people on a no health care program, suggest to me that they are in love with the American rich- only! It appeared that tax breaks for the wealthy are high on the Republican agenda.

Some Republican supporters of Number 45 pointed to 40 US counties who experienced difficulties with the implementation of the Affordable Care Act. This number interested me. So, to investigate the number, I went to Google.com and posted the question. How many counties are in the United States? The response is as follows: "As of 2013, the United States has 3,007 counties and 137 county equivalents for a total of 3,144 counties and county-equivalents. The number of counties per state ranges from the 3 in Delaware to the 254 counties of Texas. Deductive reasoning would suggest if there are a limited number of counties with ACA challenges, reparation is possible when addressed.

Rest assured that the removal of the Affordable Care Act had less to do with health care for Americans as it does with the elimination of the legacy of President Barak Obama. Number 45 may not have killed seventy men on one stone. However, on Friday, July 14, 2017, during his repeal and replace speech, his signature on a health care bill would have literally placed millions of Americans on a death path. It was man's inhumanity to man in action!

The undercurrent of nationalism during his speeches in France and Germany had even made world leaders uncomfortable. Once a respected country on the world stage, America was the center of world policies. The behavior of Number 45 physically moved the US from front row center stage to the front-row far left at the G-20 Summit meeting during summer 2017. The photo of Number 45 in Hamburg, Germany spoke volumes. Marc Champion, Peter Martin, and Brian Parkin expound on this shift in leadership. They pointed to the fact that the US is being represented by a president who promoted protectionism, abandoning decades of American cheerleading for free trade. The July 5, 2017, article in the Houston Chronicle states that China and Germany are informally being encouraged to move into a leadership role since the US-Number 45 has left a vacuum in the international trade arena. The comments made by some world leaders reflect how Number 45 was recognized on the world stage.

Argentina, President Mauricio Macri: On his former business partner, during the election:

Trump is a "totally crackpot presidential candidate," Mr. Macri said (in Spanish). "Facilitate the election of Hilary [Clinton]".

Australia, Prime Minister Malcolm Turnbull: In embarrassing leaked audio, mocking Trump in an impersonation:" Donald and I, we are winning and winning in the polls," Turnbull said in the leaked audio of him mocking Trump. "Not the fake polls! They're the ones we're not winning... I have this Russian guy..." *Brazil, Michel Termer*: On Donald Trump at the time of his election: Donald Trump's election does not "change anything... Brazil's relationship with the United States is an institutional relationship, from state to state." *Canada, Prime Minister Justin Trudeau*: "To those fleeing persecution, terror & war, Canadians will welcome you, regardless of your faith. Diversity is our strength #WelcomeToCanada."

EU, Donald Tusk: In an open letter to EU leaders, criticizing Mr. Trump: "Particularly the change in Washington puts the European Union in a difficult situation; with the new administration seeming to put into question the last 70 years of American foreign policy."

EU Commission President Jean-Claude Juncker: On leaving the Paris climate agreement:

"Mr. Trump doesn't get close enough to the dossiers to fully understand them. We tried to explain that... in clear German sentences. It seems our attempt failed." *France, President Emmanuel Macron*: On Mr. Trump leaving the Paris climate agreement: "I do think it is a mistake - both for the US and for our planet. Tonight, I wish to tell the United States, France believes in you. The world believes in you. I know that you are a great nation."

Like Abimelech-the tumble-weed king, those who oppose or who are suspected of opposing Number 45 will find themselves in a precarious position, or out of a job. Shermichael Singleton, Housing and Urban Development (HUD) official, and Republican political consultant was fired during the time Number 45 was president-elect. James Comey, FBI Director with a 10-year term, was fired as a result of his investigation of the perceived bromance relationship between

Number 45 and Russian president Vladimir Putin. As a result of not supporting his travel band against foreigners, Sally Yates was fired. Also fired was Craig Deare, National Security Council Senior Director for Western Hemisphere. Affairs. Preet Bharara, United States Attorney for the Southern District of New York was hired, then fired. I wonder if his relationship as former United States Attorney for the Southern District of New York had something to do with his firing. Others have been forced into early retirement, or just forced out. This was pointed out in the article regarding the US State Department.

If we are to examine the US as a kingdom, the United States would be divided as it once was before the Civil War. Biblically, Rehoboam divided Israel into a northern and southern kingdom. In a similar stance, Trump has sought to isolate the US by building a wall to separate the US from Mexico and the rest of the world. He also sought to isolate the US from the world by undermining 70 years of global relationships.

One of the most significant aspects of this has proven to be is the extremely hypocritical acts by the Evangelistic community as they laid hands and prayed for Number 45 while Number 45 was ready with a pen in hand to sign a bill that would prey on Americans health insurance.

On a personal note; how many presidents get a 'pass' for what they say about women, immigrants, the disabled, and foreign-born US citizens? Would President Obama be given a 'pass'? I don't think so!!

And America's downward spiral continued.

CHAPTER TEN

Closing

The entire goal of this manuscript is to point out that leadership matters! I have drawn from the events of Judges 9 from the King James Bible Old Testament and fast-forwarded those events to the current president of the United States- Number 45, Donald J. Trump. The scriptures do not provide the names of the people King Abimelech solicited to bring carnage to his people. We know that Abimelech received 70 coins from family elders. In contrast, Number 45 received a salary. As president, he used his position to hire some of the most un-American cabinet members and staff. Included are people like Steve Miller, anti-Semite, and Steve Bannon, who has a documented history of hatred for Muslims, and African Americans. (Several members had been replaced with a new set of questionable un-Americans). The actions and public statements of Donald Trump include:

- During a February 27, 2018, CNN interview with Jack Tapper, Trump stated, "He is of Mexican heritage." The Honorable Gonzalo Curiel, a federal judge, presided over the lawsuit regarding Trump University.
- Trump Plaza Hotel and Casino was fined $200,000 in 1992 by the New Jersey Casino Control Commission. Managers removed African American card dealers at the request of a big-spending gambler. A state appeals court upheld the fine.
- Trump was the leading proponent of birtherism, the racist conspiracy theory that President Barack Obama was not born in the United States and is an illegitimate president.

- Mexican immigrants are criminals and rapists.
- A white woman was beaten and raped while jogging in Manhattan Central Park. Trump took out full-page ads in four New York City newspapers calling for the return of the death penalty in New York, and the expansion of police authority. The accused were five innocent African American teenagers.
- On more than one occasion, Trump was accused of assault against women.
- The Trump corporation was sued in 1973 by the Justice Department for racial discrimination against African Americans looking to rent apartments in Brooklyn, Queens, and Staten Island. Just three years after that, the Justice Department sued the Trump Management Corporation again for allegedly discriminating against Black applicants by telling them apartments were not available.

Unfortunately, the structure built by African Americans is the resident of an unworthy and ineffective leader; however, it is a good time to be alive! On what biases can I make this statement? Americans who have experienced the actions of the current administration have come together to challenge many detrimental acts on the American public. People are coming together, white, black, brown, and yellow, for the betterment of America. They do this despite the actions and tweets of Number 45.

It would be remiss not to recognize the over two hundred and fifty million individuals who have died due to Covid19, the incompetence of Number 45 and White House supporters. Towards the end of the 20th Century, over 900 Americans committed suicide following the dictates of Jim Jones, leader of the Peoples Temple. Ownership of inactions in this 21st Century coronavirus deaths is caused by Number 45.

As Christians, we have the Bible that was written by men, and inspired by God as a guide, in addition to a moral compass. Men and women are created by God and given dominion to care for what He created. God created the Earth full of beauty and richness. He looked at His creation in Genesis 1 (31) and did not say, "This is good." He said, "This is very good!" Yet, through industrialized initiatives, the Earth is being ravished. Sinkholes occurred in certain parts of the US. The wetlands are being pushed back in Louisiana. We read that some parts of Utah have begun to have tremors and earthquakes. Some have even speculated that Nevada would eventually be the Pacific Ocean coastline. At various times it is difficult to breathe because of the polluted air.

Global warming was well-documented by Al Gore and seventeen scientists from around the world. And yet, America has succumbed to an administration that feverously argued that global warming is a hoax. To add insult to injury, Number 45 had placed an individual in a leadership position in the Environmental Protection Agency. Before being appointed, he attempted to sue the EPA on fourteen different occasions. Yet, it is a good time to be alive. I would argue that before God allows men to destroy His creation, He will do it Himself. Genesis Chapter 6 and 7 portrays the events of Noah and his family and shared what God, Himself will do when there are actions contrary to His Words!

Evangelical preachers were photographed with their hands towards Number 45 for prayer. They prayed for Number 45 as he and his political supporters preyed on Americans with regards to affordable health care, the environment, and other needed services. The Book of Leviticus, Chapter 10 (1-3) speaks to the priest (preachers) who perform acts contrary to the words of God. Joy Reid, of MSNBC AM Joy aired an interview with Rev. Dr. William Barber II:

"When we have this extremist Trump Republican agenda that takes health care, transfers wealth to the greedy, that's hypocrisy and sin.

Seven hundred billion dollars Joy, you haven't seen that kind of transfer of wealth on the backs of bodies of people since slavery. Claiming to care about life, but then passing a bill when you know thousands will die, 22 million people, poor, working people will be hurt. That is hypocrisy and sin. When you know it will hurt children, the disabled and veterans, that is a sin. That is hypocrisy" (July 21, 2017).

Through the Book of Numbers, for every blessing, the Israelites complained. 21st Century politics has shown that when a narrative causes an over-emphasis of complaints, people will bring harm to themselves. God demonstrates that there are consequences for disobedience. One possible result was the loss of affordable health care for millions of Americans, and an already defiled educational system being exasperated. Programs for youth and seniors were falling by the wayside, and much more. The demolishment of health care was a bill that was ready to be signed by Number 45 once voted on by congress. Thank God for John Mc Caine. And even though the bill did not pass, efforts were underway among Republicans to start the dismantling process again. We moved from Friday Failure to Sabotage Saturday to the Supreme Court catastrophe!

The word of God is not a toy. The Old Testament includes books that focus on laws and justice. Deuteronomy, Chapters 27 and 28, has a message for blessings and curses. America had a previous administration with a team of experts, who pushed through programs to uplift and protect all Americans. For the past four years, we had an administration with one plan and that was to dismantle the holistic programs of the previous administration. This would have brought harm to many Americans, even those who voted for Number 45. Again, the judgment is on those who voted for an unworthy leader. But God said, "If my people who are called by my name will humble themselves and pray and seek my face and turn from their wicked ways, then I will hear from heaven, and I will heal their land" (2nd Chronicle 7:14). God has thousands of blessings in His hand, just for charity. Who would not want to be alive to experience God's blessings during challenging times? The Bible states, "…And if it seems evil unto you to serve the Lord, "choose you this day who you will serve; whether the gods which your fathers served that were on the other side of the flood, or the gods of the Amorites, in whose land we dwell: but as for me and my house, we will serve the Lord, so said Joshua, Chapter 24 (15). As we reflect on the manifestation of Judges 9, in 21st Century politics, that is the question, whom do we serve?

There are many messages throughout the Book of Judges. One message is clear, as in the case of Abimelech. Judges 9 (53) shows there is not a positive end to those who seek a position not sanctioned by God and who do evil against God's people.

In this era of 21st Century politics, it is interesting, that like Israel, the US demanded a new president. And, by any means necessary, Number 45 assumed the position but not as a president. What appeared was a desire to be a dictator. For this writing, a dictator is someone "…who has absolute power, or who at least behaves as if they can do whatever they want without consequence." In 1st Samuel, we find a similar situation as the Israelites demanded a king. Verses 7 through 18 share the outcome when their desired king was anointed in the position of leadership.

Number 45 did not recommend the physical death of James Comey for his legal investigation of Number 45's Russian connection. However, he did, on a national and international scale, attempted to discredit the past director of the FBI. In 2nd Samuel, David, allowing his flesh to take power over his better judgment, arranged for Uriah's physical death. For his decision, he was charged by God for his infraction. In Chapter 12, (1-10) God sent Nathan to chastise King David. Nathan was the conduit to articulate the consequence of his actions. Who dared to be God's conscious to Number 45? Thus far, no one. What made this situation even worse is the infringement of Covid19. The deadly virus has killed over 250,000 American citizens. The unworthy leader has shown not a molecule of concern. Mitch McConnel, the Republican leader of the Senate, stands guard to ensure much needed federal financial support has no interest. He holds this position while he contaminates the judicial system with conservative judges, some found not worthy of the life-long appointment. American citizens: parents, grandparents, children, colleagues, family members are dead while Number 45 and McConnell execute authority to hamper and hurt Americans.

America is advanced citizenship that requires certain qualities. In leadership, these salient qualities include but are not limited to, intelligence, clarity of thought and processes, a moral compass, empathy, wisdom, discernment, and a heart for God and his people. These qualities are required above all else. 1st King, in the Bible, portrays the newly appointed King Solomon. In chapters 3 and 4, he had the sense to recognize that ruling required wisdom. In verse 9, Solomon asked God for an understanding mind and a sensitive heart to judge and to discern between good and bad. As Pastor West stated, we live in a society of checks and balances. As such, there is no king. However, a president may take on the persona of a king, or dictator as he promotes himself and his children as a ruling class.

When we look at the American check and balance system, we see the illegal efforts to ensure that millions of individuals will not be allowed to cast their vote. Gerrymandering and attempts at voter suppression are at an all-time high. This latest attempt to develop a centralized voting collection hub with personal information jeopardizes American's privacy. Here again, it appears that there is an attempt made by the Number 45 administration to hand over America to Russia, or a like-minded country.

In the 2nd Kings, we see Elijah and Elisha, one leader and one subordinate. Elijah set standards based on God's principles for Elisha to follow. In contrast, the message from Trump is not to set an example or to be a guide. Instead, the norm has become to pass the buck and not take responsibility for your actions. All the accolades are accepted, even when you have not done the work. For example, the increase in employment that was implemented under the Obama administration is a good example. One phrase that cannot be understated; it is the administrator who set the tone, regardless of the type of institution.

1st and 2nd Chronicles focused on two themes: God's covenant with David and the temple. These books show the temple of God as the main location of interest. David planed it. Solomon built it. Kings were crowned in it. Prophets were killed in it, and the law was re-discovered in it. In these books, we see an illustration of worthy and unworthy kings. Out of all the kings in the Old Testament, only five were found to be worthy. They include King Abijah, King Jehoshaphat, King Jotham, King Hezekiah, and King Josiah. Although they had wealth, they were men of valor and the ability to be victorious in battle. They followed the instruction of God-not man.

King Asa, King Rehoboam, King Uzziah, King Manasseh, King Jehoram, King Ahaziah, Queen Athaliah, King Amaziah, King Ahaz, King Amon, King Jehoiakim, King Jehoahaz, King Jehoiachin. and King Zedekiah consulted other gods, made bad decisions, and some killed their children and grandchildren. These were unworthy leaders who found a terrible end to their lives and reign.

Ezra and Nehemiah are books used to illustrate what had been built and torn down can be re-built, rather than repealed and replaced. Being challenged by enemies should never be a deterrent when a task is required by God. When you lose your way, go back, get back in line, and do what is correct in God's eyes. This can only happen if the person recognizes that they are out of line. God told Jeremiah to tell us all, in 29: 11-13, "For I know the thoughts that I think toward you, saith the Lord; thoughts of peace, and not of evil, to give you an expected end. (12) Then shall you call upon me and ye shall go and pray unto me and

I will hearken unto thee. (13) And ye shall seek me and find me. When ye shall search for me with all your heart."

As stated, there is a very old saying that if you dig one ditch, you had better dig two. For the ditch, you dig, just maybe for you. Ester, in the book that bears her name, provides another example of leadership. there was one vicious man, Haman; one weak King, Ahasuerus; the quiet wisdom of one man, Mordecai, and the courage of a young woman, Ester. Leadership requires that you look beyond yourself and serve the people God has entrusted to you. And, it is a reminder to not disparage or dig ditches for those who oppose you.

I would suggest that only a true Christian would have a clear understanding that the plight of Job is not about Job, but about Satan's attempt to embarrass God. God is sovereign, and He can do whatever He chooses. A leader must be steadfast and unmovable during good and bad times. Psalms and Proverbs are songs of praise and words of wisdom. These books were written primarily by King David, and his son Solomon. These leaders were and are examples of what to do in times of uncertainty, mistakes, sins, and confusion, and who we are to turn. They also provide a path to get back into God's grace.

In this era of proposed nationalism, the words of Ecclesiastes become paramount. The section portion of Chapter 4 verse 10 states, "…but woe to him that is alone when he falleth; for he hath not another to help him up." I am not making an indictment. What I am saying is if you build a wall on the premise that you are keeping so-called undesirable out, you will also be keeping in undesirables. If you dismiss international relations that have been a staple for seven decades of positive and effective relationships, and interactions, you may just find yourself alone. As a country, America could not afford to be without allies. The problem with an unworthy leader is that millions of people will be affected.

During the Obama presidency we found no scandals and no extramarital affairs. Instead, we found a love and a friendship between the first lady and the president. Publicly, their hands became one. Their relationship cannot be denied. And all indications suggest that they have a love for God and a love of man and woman-human kind. As I read Song of Solomon, I reflected on the love Jesus has for mankind. When among the most ardent of racist and mean-spirited situations, Obama put forth policies, programs, and an agenda to improve the quality of life for all Americans. With regards to the planet, he negotiated and held a leadership position with the Paris Peace Agreement.

After June 2017

In the Preface, I stated, we will understand by and by. What do we understand? As of Monday, September 28, 2020, we understand the Donald J Trump shows, according to the New York Times report, that he has unpaid taxes. He is millions of dollars in debt. The question is, who is he indebted to? Why is that important? I suspect much of the money he owes is to President Putin. His son had bragged that they can get all the money they want from Russia. Tina Nguyen, May 8, 2017, in an article in Vanity Fair magazine quotes, Eric Trump, "We don't rely on American banks. We have all the funding we need out of Russia." Could that be the reason why he continues to throw American judicial institutions under the bus? Early in Trump's presidency, David Corn's December 14, 2016, in an article in Mother Jones magazine states, "It is nearly certain that [Russian intelligence] would have done some sort of surveillance on him. Could it have been low-key physical surveillance (following etc.) or deeper surveillance, such as video/audio of hotel room and monitoring of electronics (your [communications] while [in Moscow] is on their network)." American businessmen as guests are a particular interest. Could there be footage of Trump in one of the Russian hotels that show his behavior? It would not be a surprise to learn that he and his family are subject to the dictates of Russian oligarchs who are subjects to President Putin. For President Putin, his dogs wear his collar! Is he beholding to someone? And is Trump, the president of the United States, a conduit for Russia? Could his behavior place the US under foreign rule?

What do we understand? We understand that Trump has alleged disrespect for women. Eliza Relman, September 17, 2020, the article in Business Insider; The 26 women who have accused Trump of sexual misconduct.

- At least 26 women have accused President Donald Trump of sexual misconduct since the 1970s.
- Renewed attention was brought to the allegations amid the #MeToo movement and a national conversation concerning sexual misconduct.
- Trump has repeatedly denied the accusations, denouncing his accusers as "liars."
- In June 2019, columnist E. Jean Carroll accused President Donald Trump of sexually assaulting her by forcing his penis inside her in a Bergdorf Goodman dressing room in the mid-1990s.
- And in September 2020, model Amy Dorris said that in 1997 Trump forcibly kissed her, groped her all over her body, and gripped her tightly so she couldn't getaway.

What do we understand? We understand without question that Donald Trump is a racist. His public statements can be seen in the David A. Graham, Adrienne Green, Cullen Murphy, and Parker Richards, June 2019 article, "An Oral History of Trump's Bigotry" His racism and intolerance has always been in evidence; only slowly did he begin to understand how to use them to his advantage. What is most disturbing is the separation of immigrant families. The pictures of children in cages are hard to forget.

In the years since then, Trump has assembled a long record of comments on issues involving African Americans as well as Mexicans, Hispanics more broadly, Native Americans, Muslims, Jews, immigrants, women, and people with disabilities. His statements have been reflected in his behavior—from public acts (placing ads calling for the execution of five young black and Latino men accused of rape, who were later shown to be innocent) to private preferences ("When Donald and Ivana came to the casino, the bosses would order all the black people off the floor," a former employee of Trump's Castle, in Atlantic City, New Jersey, told a writer for The New Yorker).

What do we understand? In my estimation, Trump has pushed this country into a position of isolation. America First has moved to America alone. Cfr.com presents a timeline from 2017 to 2020, Trump's Foreign Policy Moments. It states, "Donald J. Trump's presidency has marked a profound departure from U.S. leadership in areas such as trade and diplomacy, as well as an across-the-board toughening of immigration policies.

What do we understand? We understand that Trump's incompetence and arrogance have caused the death of over 270,700 Americans. Cfr. com states, on March 13, 2020, National Emergency Over Coronavirus.

After initially downplaying the risk of a new coronavirus disease, COVID-19, Trump declared a national emergency as a case ballooned. The move unlocks roughly $50 billion in federal funding and allows the loosening of some regulations on health-care providers. Trump also announces new efforts to boost coronavirus testing, after what many see as an anemic federal response, and later signs more than $2 trillion in economic stimulus legislation. Trump increasingly blames China, where the virus originated, for misleading the world and threatens retaliation.

What do we understand? Trump with the assistance of Mitch McConnell, who showed absolute hypocrisy with the Supreme Court nomination with justice Garland now is aggressively pushing forward with an individual who will push back a woman's right to choose and the possible loss of health care for millions of Americans.

And so, America has lost its footings around the world and many, many Americans are losing or will lose. If we ever needed an example that leadership matters, we can look to Donald J. Trump who has proven to be the least most effective person in leadership.

Is God so disgusted with America that He is bringing judgment on his people?

On January 20, 2021, President-elect Joseph Biden will be the 47th President of the United States. I hope and pray that he will be able to bring our fragmented country back together. While Obama brought out the best of American citizens; Trump brought out the absolute worst of Americans.

We must be mindful and diligent and recognize that there is always a Trump type behavior waiting in the wings with supporters seeking to establish an ungodly union.

I felt this would be an opportunity to say thank you to my pastor, Rev. Dr. Ralph West, Pastor of The Church Without Walls, Houston, Texas, and to share a little about myself. From an early age, church involvement has been a large aspect of my life. Baptized at the age of 8 at the Morning Star Baptist Church in Buffalo, New York, my mother insisted that we attend Sunday School classes. After moving from public housing into a home, we quickly joined a neighborhood church. From age 15 onward, Antioch Missionary Baptist Church was my home church for nearly 44 years. I ventured to Mt. Ararat Missionary Baptist Church for a few years but returned to my home church. Rev. Guy J. Graves preached, married my x-husband and me, and funeralized some of my family members.

After completing my education, I packed my SUV and relocated to Houston, Texas. I can recall driving through South West Houston on a Sunday because I had heard on TSU, 90.9 FM radio, that there was an evening service at The Church Without Walls. At that time, I could not recall the name of the church, but I remembered hearing the street. So, of course, I went about asking people to direct me to Queenston Blvd. At that time, I was living in South West Houston, seeking the church which is in North West Houston. I was asking the wrong people for a church in a different section of the city. My daughter had relocated and found the church. And, as soon as I learned the address, I found the church; and on a Friday evening, when another preacher had given the sermon, I joined. And I have not looked back.

We are required as Christians to worship and praise God, and I do. And, I thank my pastor for his leadership. Pastor West does what God has instructed; feed His sheep! God gives him His best, and in turn, he gives us his best. Even in his absence, which is seldom; he has the best preachers in his stead. I have learned that it does not take-away the attributes from one to give another a compliment. Jesus comes first!

Pastor West and his family are strong examples for members and visitors alike. His teaching stands in the realm of being God's ultimate change agent. Under his leadership, ungodly behaviors were minimized or eliminated. And, behaviors change for the good. He is the ultimate example that leadership does matter.

Thank you, Pas!

REFERENCES

Ackerson, John. (April 29, 2017) Interview Trump 100 days in office:

Baker, Peter. (2017). Conspiracy or Coincidence? A Timeline Open to Interpretation. New York Times-News Online

Business Dictionary. (2014). 5th edition. Boston MA: Houghton Mifflin Harcourt Publisher

CBS News. (2017). A timeline surrounding Donald Trump Jr.'s meeting with Russian lawyer. New York: New York Times News

Chite, Nate. (2017). Obamacare is not in a death spiral. New York: Fact Check

_____ (2017). Consumer Report. Yonker, NY: Consumer Union LLC Compton, A. (November 11, 2017) Ann Compton Reports. ABC News

Cooper, Helen, and Schmitt, Eric. (2016). Trump's Cabinet. New York: New York Times

Engle, Richard, (7/21/2017). Russia. MSNBC

Face the Nation CBS News. Interview with Vice president Mike Pence

Fact Check. Org. (2008-9/19/2006). Philadelphia, PA: Annenberg Public Policy Center

Harper, Steven. (2017). A timeline: Russia and President Trump. New York: Moyer and Company

Jacobson, Louis (2017). Donald Trump boasts about accomplishments in the officering hollow. New York: New York Times News Online

King James Version. (1994). The Holy Bible. Nashville, TN: Thomas Nelson Publishers Ye Hee Lee. M. (2016) Jeff Session comments on race. For the record. () The Fact Checker

Leonhardt D. & Thompson, A. (2017). Trump Lies. New York: New York Times News Online

Letterman, D. (10/17/2013) The David Letterman Show. Donald Trump Interview

Levitz, Eric. (2017). All the terrifying things that Donald Trump did lately. New York: New York Magazine.

Maddow. R. (October 30, 2016). Rachel Maddow Show. MSNBC

Maddow. R. 9 November 3, 2016). Rachel Maddow show. MSNBC

Mc Coy, Kevin. (1/23/2017). Aetna-Humana $37B merger blocked over fear it would harm consumers. USA Today News Online.

Miller, E. F. & Winston, K. (12/13/16) Religion News Service. Cabinet: Trump Advisers: The Faith Factor.

Mosberger. D. (2107). Scott Pruitt has sued the Environmental Protection Agency 13 Times, now he wants to lead it. New York: Huff Post

Murray, David. (2017). Head Heart Hand Blog

Myers, Joyce. (2006). Notes and Commentary. Holy Bible. New York: Warner Faith Publisher

New York Times. (February 14, 2017). Members of trump Cabinet

New York Times. (April 5, 20170. The Russia Story, a Total Hoax

Obama, B.H. (1/9/2009). Affordable Health Care Act speech. CBS News Online Oxford Dictionary.

Paris, Carol, Ph.D. (2017). Tom Price as HHS Secretary: A Disaster for U.S. Health Care. Portland ME: Common Dreams Publicans

Pew Research. (2017). Washington, D.C. Bergmann, Max (6/29/2017). Present at the Destruction: How Rex Tillerson is destroying the State Department. Politico Magazine.

Reid, Joy, (7/22/2017- 10:00 am) AM Joy Morning Show. MSNBC

Rozzer, Matthew. (5/15/2017). Mick Mulvany gets schooled about diabetes after saying, "It's caused by poor lifestyle choices." New York: MSNBC News

Ruper, Aaron. (2107). Mulvany, "We must lower the debt for unborn children by taking food from existing children. Think Progress: (city/state):

Stephanopoulos, G. (April 13, 2017). Carter Page Interview. ABC Morning Show

Strauss, Valerie. (2016). A sobering look at what Betsy De Vos did to educate in Michigan- and what she might do as Secretary of Education. New York: Bloomberg News Publishers

Swift, Art. (2015). Gallup. Putin's image rises in the US. Mostly among Republicans. Gallup Poll.

St. John. Allen. (5/2/2017). How the Affordable Care Act drove down personal bankruptcy.

The Associated Press. (April 17, 2017) Paul Manaford

Todd, C. (February 26, 2017). Meet the Press. Chuck Todd notes a pattern with Donald Trump

Utell, Janine. (2017). Widener University, Pennsylvania

Washington Post. (February 13, 2017) Sally Yates Warns the White House

Washington Post. (March 21, 2016). Trump Identifies Carter Page as Policy Advisor Washington Post. (April 17, 2017)

Wall Street Journal. (March 30, 2017). Report on Mike Flynn

Weill, K. (2/15/17). Innocent Man Finally Pardoned After Mike Pence Refused to Clear His Name. Daily Beast online.

Wheeler, Brian (2017). What is Marx's Das Kapital? UK: UK Politics

Wootson, C. R. Jr. (2016). Several pastors prayed over President Trump. Another one says, they border on hypocrisy. The Washington Post News. p. 73-74

Printed in the United States
By Bookmasters